Edward Miall

Title-deeds of the Church of England to the Parochial Endowments

Edward Miall

Title-deeds of the Church of England to the Parochial Endowments

ISBN/EAN: 9783337000790

Printed in Europe, USA, Canada, Australia, Japan

Cover: Foto ©Lupo / pixelio.de

More available books at **www.hansebooks.com**

TITLE-DEEDS

OF

THE CHURCH OF ENGLAND

TO HER

PAROCHIAL ENDOWMENTS.

LONDON
PRINTED BY SPOTTISWOODE AND CO.
NEW-STREET SQUARE

TITLE-DEEDS

OF

THE CHURCH OF ENGLAND

TO HER

PAROCHIAL ENDOWMENTS.

BY

EDWARD MIALL.

LONDON:
LONGMAN, GREEN, LONGMAN, AND ROBERTS.
1862.

PREFACE.

The principal aim of the writer in collecting and putting together the information contained in the following pages has been to clear away certain factitious and mischievous obstructions to the free course of dispassionate discussion of one of the gravest questions of the present day— the religious propriety and political expediency of maintaining a national Church Establishment. It has been found almost impossible to argue the negative view of that question, but especially to base upon that view any direct political action, without being indignantly assailed as making an attempt to subvert the rights of property. Cries of "spoliation," "robbery," "sacrilege," and the like, have been instantly raised to cut short the argument, or to bury political effort beneath an overwhelming weight of scornful vituperation. Men anxious, above all things, to see in these realms a free Church, self-governed and self-sustaining, and taking such practical steps towards the realisation of their desire as might best commend themselves to their judgment, have been charged, almost as a matter of course, with wishing to wrest from the Church of England — meaning by the term, the prelates, clergy, and professed members of that Church,— endowments which are as much her or their property, as the best titled estates of any landowner in the kingdom. These endowments are always assumed to rest upon the same foundation as those in the possession of the various denominations of Dissenters; and all proposals to deal with them with the same freedom as other national property may be dealt with are eagerly denounced as confiscation.

The immediate purpose of the writer of the following treatise has been to remove the misconception upon which this demurrer to all calm and fair discussion of the great question at issue is based. Those who urge the dissolution of the union between Church and State may have embraced erroneous principles, or may be utterly mistaken in their anticipation of the religious effect that would result from their universal adoption — and if so, the more dispassionate the controversy, the sooner and the more completely will their error be exposed. But as long as they are treated as would-be spoliators, greedy of what belongs to others, and tenacious of what they claim as their own, the contest will remain simply one of power, not of reason nor of faith. It is hoped that the following pages, by giving a clear view both of the facts and of the law relating to parochial tithe endowments, may help to shift the argument between the supporters and opponents of the State Church to a much higher ground; and that, at no very remote period from the present, the question will be, not as to who may be the rightful owner of the property, but as to how it may be best applied to the service of man and the glory of God.

The Firs, Upper Norwood:
Dec. 5th, 1861.

CONTENTS.

CHAPTER I.

INTRODUCTORY AND EXPLANATORY.

OBJECT OF THE TREATISE. — THE CHURCH NOT SEPARATE FROM THE STATE. — MODERN ASSUMPTIONS. — NATURE OF CHURCH PROPERTY. — SCOPE OF THE INVESTIGATION. — STATEMENT OF THE PRINCIPLE.
Pages 1—6

CHAPTER II.

RISE OF THE TITHE SYSTEM IN THE WESTERN EMPIRE.

THE APOSTOLIC CHURCH KNEW NOTHING OF TITHES. — MODE OF SUPPORTING THE CHURCH IN APOSTOLIC TIMES. — FIRST OPINION RESPECTING THE DUTY TO PAY TITHES. — TITHES PAYABLE ONLY IN THE WESTERN CHURCH. — THE COUNCIL OF MAÇON. — SPECIAL CONSECRATION OF TITHE BY ROYAL AUTHORITY IN THE EIGHTH CENTURY. — THE GROUNDWORK OF TITHES TO BE FOUND IN THE LAWS OF CHARLEMAGNE. — THE LAW REMAINED FOR MANY YEARS A DEAD LETTER . . . 7—13

CHAPTER III.

TITHES IN ENGLAND. — THEIR ORIGIN IN LAW.

FIRST AUTHORITY FOR PAYMENT OF TITHES EXCLUSIVELY ECCLESIASTICAL. — LAWS OF OFFA. — LAWS OF ETHELWOLF. — THE LAW OF ETHELWOLF THE FOUNDATION OF THE CIVIL RIGHT TO TITHES. — LAWS OF ALFRED. — LAWS OF ATHELSTAN. — LAWS OF EDMUND. — LAWS OF EDGAR. — LAWS OF ETHELRED. — LAWS OF CANUTE. — LAWS OF WILLIAM THE CONQUEROR.

—OATH OF THE NORMAN KINGS TO OBSERVE THE LAWS OF EDWARD THE CONFESSOR.—SUCH A SUCCESSION OF LAWS A PROOF OF PUBLIC ORIGIN OF TITHES . . . . . . Pages 14—26

CHAPTER IV.

LAY RECUSANCY IN REGARD TO TITHES.

UNWILLINGNESS OF THE LAITY TO PAY TITHES. — CONDITION OF THE PEOPLE WHEN THE TITHE SYSTEM WAS ESTABLISHED. — THE TITHE LAWS CANNOT BE ACCOUNTED FOR ON THE THEORY OF THE PRIVATE ORIGIN OF TITHES. — ENLARGEMENT OF ECCLESIASTICAL DEMANDS. — TRIPARTITE DIVISION OF TITHES.—ITS ABANDONMENT.—NEW CLAIMS. — PROOF FROM THESE FACTS THAT TITHES ARE THE PRODUCT OF PUBLIC LAW.—NECESSITY FOR THE LAW FROM THE INDISPOSITION OF THE LAITY.—ANATHEMAS AGAINST RECUSANTS . . . 27—37

CHAPTER V.

THINGS LEGALLY TITHEABLE.

PRÆDIAL TITHES: GREAT.—PRÆDIAL TITHES: SMALL.—MIXED TITHES.— PERSONAL TITHES. — OBSERVATIONS ON THINGS TITHEABLE. — THE RANGE OF THE CLAIM TO TITHES A PROOF OF THEIR PUBLIC ORIGIN. — CHARACTER OF PERSONAL TITHES A PROOF OF THEIR PUBLIC ORIGIN . . . . 38—54

CHAPTER VI.

MODERN EXPANSION AND EXTENSION OF TITHE ENDOWMENTS.

CERTAIN PROPORTION OF TITHES DERIVED FROM THE PRODUCE OF THE SOIL. — EXTENT OF LAND UNDER CULTIVATION IN THIS COUNTRY. — OPERATION OF THE ENCLOSURE BILLS.—PROPORTION OF LAND UNDER CULTIVATION WHEN THE BARREN LAND ACT OF EDWARD VI. WAS PASSED.—OPERATION OF THIS ACT.—AREA OF CULTIVATED GROUND IN THE REIGN OF KING JOHN. — EIGHT-NINTHS OF TITHE PROPERTY DIRECTLY TRACED TO THEIR SOURCE IN PUBLIC LAW.—OBJECTIONS ANTICIPATED.—ABSURDITY OF THE PRIVATE THEORY . 55—64

CHAPTER VII.

ARBITRARY ASSIGNMENT OF TITHES.

REASONS FOR THE PRIVATE THEORY EXAMINED. — STRUGGLE BETWEEN PUBLIC AUTHORITY AND PRIVATE RIGHT IN THE MIDDLE AGES.—THE OBLIGATION TO PAY TITHES WAS ONE OF THE RESULTS OF THIS

STRUGGLE.—THE RIGHT OF ARBITRARY CONSECRATION OF TITHES WAS HOWEVER RETAINED. — EFFECTS OF ARBITRARY CONSECRATION. — POSITION OF THE LAND OWNER.—HOW TITHES WERE APPORTIONED.— RETENTION OF TITHES BY LAYMEN.—ESTABLISHMENT OF THE SYSTEM OF APPROPRIATIONS. — DIFFERENCE OF TITLE TO APPROPRIATED AND NON-APPROPRIATED TITHES. — OSTENSIBLE OBJECTS OF APPROPRIATION. —ANCIENT INSTRUMENT OF APPROPRIATION. — ARBITRARY CONSECRATIONS DID NOT AFFECT THE LEGAL ORIGIN OF THE PROPERTY. — THEY WERE FROM PARISH CHURCHES, NOT TO THEM. — NO PARISH CHURCHES BECAME POSSESSED OF TITHES BY DEED. — THE STATUTES OF DISSOLUTION.—TITHES AND CHURCH RATES.—PROBABLE ORIGIN OF CHURCH RATES . . . . Pages 65—83

CHAPTER VIII.

CONDITIONS OF USUFRUCT PRESCRIBED BY LAW.

CLAIM OF THE ESTABLISHED CHURCH.—CHURCH PROPERTY HAS ALWAYS BEEN HELD FROM THE STATE. — PROOFS OF THIS FROM PUBLIC LAWS. — THE CHURCH HAS NO CONTROL OVER ANY ECCLESIASTICAL ENDOWMENTS.—CHANGES OF USE IN CHURCH PROPERTY.—CHURCH PROPERTY HELD ON CONDITIONS . . . . 84—95

CHAPTER IX.

GENERAL CONCLUSIONS.

THE CHURCH NOT DISTINGUISHABLE FROM THE PEOPLE. — THE CHURCH IS NOT A CORPORATION.— THE CHURCH HAS NO EXCLUSIVE RIGHTS.— THE CHURCH THE CREATURE OF THE STATE. — THE PAROCHIAL ENDOWMENTS OF THE CHURCH ORIGINATED IN PUBLIC LAW. — CHURCH PROPERTY IS NATIONAL PROPERTY . . . . . 95—102

SUPPLEMENTARY CHAPTER.

OCCASION FOR WRITING THIS TREATISE.— MISAPPREHENSIONS AS TO THE NATURE OF CHURCH PROPERTY. — SELDEN ON THE PUBLIC ORIGIN OF TITHES. — EDINBURGH REVIEW ON THE CHURCH NOT A CORPORATION. — LORD BROUGHAM DITTO.— LORD HARDWICKE ON THE RELATION OF THE CLERGY TO THE STATE. — SIR JAMES MACKINTOSH ON CHURCH PROPERTY. — LORD CAMPBELL DITTO. — LORD MELBOURNE DITTO. — LORD ALTHORP DITTO.— LORD PALMERSTON DITTO.— LORD MACAULAY DITTO.— EDINBURGH REVIEW DITTO. — DEAN MILMAN ON THE ORIGIN

OF TITHES.—REV. J. C. ROBERTSON DITTO.—FULLER DITTO.—BISHOP STILLINGFLEET DITTO.—AYLIFFE DITTO.—BISHOP WATSON, BISHOP WARBURTON, AND THE REV. ISAAC TAYLOR ON THE RIGHTS OF THE STATE WITH RESPECT TO CHURCH PROPERTY . Pages 103—118

APPENDIX — THE TITHE COMMUTATION ACT . 119—164

INDEX . . . . 165—167

TITLE DEEDS OF THE CHURCH OF ENGLAND
TO HER PAROCHIAL ENDOWMENTS.

CHAPTER I.

INTRODUCTORY AND EXPLANATORY.

THE simple object of this treatise is to examine the title which the Church of England, " as by law established," has to the exclusive possession of the ecclesiastical endowments which, in every parish in this kingdom, are set apart for the maintenance of her clergy.

In discussing this question, it will be necessary, at the outset, to clear away, by careful definition, a cause of perpetual misunderstanding on this subject. Our inquiry will be, whether such and such property primarily belongs to the Church of England. Now, there are two senses in which that descriptive title may be interpreted. Down to comparatively modern times, the *Church* of England meant the whole body of the people of England, as *religiously* organised, just as the *State* or the Commonwealth of England meant the whole body of the people of England, as *politically* organised. This is still the legal signification of the term. But this is not the sense in which the title is popularly used in our day. When the Church of England, or the Church as by law established, is now spoken of, it is usually meant to designate that body of persons in this realm who constitute a religious community on the basis of a professed agreement in the articles, creeds, formularies, offices, and rubric, set forth in the Book of Common Prayer, and authorised by the Act of Uniformity. This religious community may be looked at, with a view to logical distinction, as apart from the State — but it is always to be borne in mind, as a matter of historic fact, that, in this country, it never had a separate existence from the State, and it is only in virtue of this connexion that it can pretend to its national title. At any rate, it is in this limited sense that the phrase has come to be employed in the present day — and it must be borne in mind, throughout, that the question about to be discussed relates to the title which *this communion*, thus defined, and thus connected, has to the ample possessions which are claimed for it exclusively.

It has become necessary to institute such an examination *afresh* — afresh, we say, because it has more than once been done before, and that by men of extraordinary ability and learning. Indeed, the fields of history, ecclesiastical literature, canon and civil law, old chartularies and other muniments, have been indefatigably traversed, and keenly scanned, in search of whatever might throw light upon the question, and the results set forth most conscientiously in works which may be found in any tolerable library. But not one man in ten thousand looks into these old treatises — has scarcely heard, perhaps, so much as their authors' names. While, on the other hand, there are thousands of clergymen, supposed by the public to be well read in the subject, who, by dint of unhesitating assumption and perpetual iteration, strive to produce an impression — an impression in which we are charitably bound to believe most of them ignorantly share — that the researches of the learned in past ages have settled the question of ownership as between the people and the Church, in favour of the latter. This assumption has, at length, got beyond the bounds of decency — insomuch that in these days Churchmen whose historic statements go right in the teeth of an overwhelming mass of historic evidence, take upon themselves to sneer at the want of information of which those are presumed to be guilty who do not receive as incontrovertible, *dicta*, as unfounded as they are modern, which but a few hundred years ago would have been but too thankfully insisted upon but for their preposterous baselessness. It is time that these hollow but loud-sounding assumptions should be brought to the test, and whatever they are worth will plainly enough appear, after a thorough and honest investigation of the Church's title-deeds.

The great bulk of Church endowments in this country consists of rent charges, or, in other words, commuted tithes. The Tithe Commutation Act, not yet thirty years of age, altered the mode of assessing and collecting the annual value, but did not in any way affect the tenure, of this kind of property. The ownership and the conditions of use remain precisely what they were before the Act was passed. The adoption of the term "rent-charge," however, in lieu of "tithes," has very materially contributed to the spread of the notion that the payments with which individuals are in the habit of voluntarily charging their landed estates, as a provision for different branches of their families, or in compensation for some service performed, and the payments which are now annually made to beneficed clergymen under that name, are analogous. It will be seen hereafter, how far such is the case. But, in order that it may be seen clearly, it will be necessary to lay aside the modern term and revert to the old one. It is principally of TITHES that it is intended to speak in the present treatise — not, indeed, to the entire exclusion of other Church possessions, which, after all, are held, for the most part, by the same tenure — but because the main question will be governed by the conclusions arrived at on this branch of it. Parochial tithes constitute, in point of fact, *the* provision for the pecuniary support of the Church of England. Episcopal and capitular estates are but buttresses to strengthen the main fabric, large, it is true, as compared with their use, but small in comparison of the entire amount of Church revenue. But so far as regards the Church "as by law established," the right to both rests upon the same foundation.

One word more by way of preliminary explanation. A full constitutional and equitable *right* to dispose of the bulk of what is called Church property as, in its wisdom, it shall at any time see fit, is about to be claimed for the Imperial Parliament. This will be the sole object of the following sections. The *expediency* of any particular set of measures grounded on such right will be left wholly untouched. An heir-at-law, by prosecuting to the utmost his claims, as such, before a legal tribunal, does not thereby preclude himself from acting with generous consideration towards the party in wrongful possession, when his title to his estate has been recognised and established. The present investigation is exclusively directed towards the settlement of the question of title — and it is clearly inexpedient to mix up with this question any considerations which ought to, and probably will, affect parliamentary action growing out of it. The first is an abstract issue — the second a practical. As to the first, we shall claim all that is due — as to the second, we shall refrain from making a single remark which will commit us to any particular course whether of demand or concession. But it should be fully understood that the establishment of a right does not necessarily imply a rigid enforcement of it. What we *may* do if we please, and what we shall *please* to do if we may, ought not to be confounded as if they were one and the same thing. Very probably they will be — but, in the very outset of this inquiry, we record our protest against it.

The general proposition, then, which it will be the

object of this treatise to establish respecting PAROCHIAL tithes, lately commuted into rent-charges, may be thus stated — *that, regarded as property separated for public religious uses, from the rest of the property of this country, they are the product of public law exclusively, ecclesiastical, or civil, or both, and that they neither did, nor, in the nature of things, could originate in private individual liberality.* It is only by a figure of speech that they can be called "endowments." They may be more properly described as an ancient "tax," the obligation to pay which sprung out of public authority, the destination of which was prescribed by public authority modified by practice, the limits and privileges of which were from time to time laid down by public authority, and the enforcement of which has, in the last resort, depended upon courts in which public authority is enthroned. In other words, tithe property was created by public law, was assigned to its uses by public law, was regulated as to what should constitute it, and to whom it either might be, or must be appropriated by public law, and, finally, was exacted from recusants by processes of public law. In England (whatever may have been the case in the Western Empire on the continent) individual spontaneity never had room to play in the creation of liability to tithe. That liability was, from the beginning of the system, fixed upon every subject of the realm, not by his own election, in obedience to pious impulses, but by the will of those who had rule over him in Church and State.

CHAP. II.

RISE OF THE TITHE SYSTEM IN THE WESTERN EMPIRE.

A VERY cursory glance at the rise and progress of the tithe system in the Western Church, from the time of the Apostles down to the first civil law for the imposition of tithes made by Charlemagne about the latter end of the eighth century, will prepare us for an intelligent survey of its origin in this country.

The history may be sketched in few words. The Christian Church knew nothing of tithes for above four hundred years after the ascension of her Lord to the throne of his spiritual kingdom.[1] During apostolic days all her temporal wants were amply supplied by the spontaneous liberality of her disciples. Each Church had its common fund, to which, at first, weekly, and afterwards, monthly contributions were made as the grace of God inclined, and ability enabled, its several members.[2] But the fund was

---

[1] Selden's "History of Tithes," chap. iv. *passim.* His conclusion is, "Till towards the end of the first four hundred (years) no *payment* of them can be proved to have been in use." Sect. 1, p. 35. Original edition 1618.

[2] Acts ii. 44 ; iv. 32, 34, 35 ; Rom. xx. 26 ; 1 Cor. xvi. 1, 2 ; 2 Cor. viii. 4 ; ix. 12. Tertullian, the eminent apologist for Christianity thus writes : " The services of God are free of any pecuniary charge. If there be any fund it is not amassed by a burdensome impost, as of a bribed superstition ; but *each person presents a moderate contribution every month*, when he chooses, and provided his inclination thus prompts

not exclusively, probably not even mainly, devoted to the maintenance of the ministry.[1] Special managers of this fund were appointed, under a designation which, in our language, may be best represented by the term "stewards," and so ample was it that, notwithstanding the Roman laws (until the times of Maxentius and Constantine) forbad the gift or bequest by will of real estates to any college, society, or corporation[2], the means of the Church were so affluent that Roman emperors could hit upon no shorter expedient for raising money than that of laying hands upon the accumulated offerings of the faithful.[3] During more than half this period, the introduction of the tithe system would have operated as a restriction on the liberality of Christian disciples.

Towards the end of the fourth century, when the clergy had become partially corrupt, and the laity less disposed to minister to their wealth, *an opinion* was here and there broached, but still in hesitating terms, that God required of his people the devotion of *a tenth*, at least, of each individual's gain, to pious uses.[4] And where this opinion was preached, as it

---

him, and his circumstances allow. For none is compelled, but each offers cheerfully. These are, as it were, the deposits of piety." Apologetic. c. 39.

[1] Acts vi. 1. Father Paul Sarpi on Benefices, chap. v.

[2] "Collegium, si nullo speciali privilegio subnixum sit, hæreditatem capere non posse dubium non est." Lex viii. *De heredibus instituendis.* Cod. lib. vi. Tit. xxiv.

[3] Father Paul Sarpi on Benefices, chap. iii.

[4] The Fathers who at this period spoke of the Christian obligation of paying tithes, were S. Ambrose, S. Augustine, S. Jerome and S. Chrysostom. We need hardly cumber our pages with extracts. They may be found set forth at length, and learnedly commented upon, in chap. v. of Selden's "History of Tithes."

was in some places, and by some bishops, it gradually consolidated into the shape of Church *doctrine*, and more or less influenced the conduct of pious laymen. But it is specially observable, that the claim then made for tithe, was that they were due " to the poor."[1] That the doctrine, however, could not have been generally received, nor the practice of offering tithe established, until after the old Roman empire, comprehending both East and West, had been severed by the successive incursions of the Goths, is clear from the fact, that the Eastern Church never once sanctioned it, and has not resorted to it down to this day.[2]

It was in the Western Church only that the system, first broached as an opinion, then elevated by the clergy to the rank of a Christian doctrine, ever reached the maturity of a Church *Law*. To France is said to belong the questionable honour of having placed the system upon this high pedestal. About A.D. 586 (in the reign of King Guntheram) a Provincial Council, attended by all the bishops of his kingdom, was held at Maçon.[3] At this council, it was ordained, as agreeable to the " Divine law," that all the people should bring in their ecclesiastical tithes, from which the priests might devote what is

---

[1] Father Paul Sarpi on Benefices, chap. vi.; Selden, chap. v. and chap. vi. sect. 6. They were commonly spoken of about the year 800, as *Res Dominicæ, Dominica substantia, Dei census, patrimonia pauperum, tributa egentium animarum, stipendia pauperum, hospitum, peregrinorum.* And according to the Council of Nantes, the clergy were bound to use them, " *non quasi suis, sed quasi commendatis.*"

[2] Father Paul on Benefices, chap. xi.; Selden, chap. v. sect. 6.

[3] Selden, chap. v. sect. 1.

required for the use of the poor, or the redemption of captives, and by their prayers obtain peace and salvation for the people.[1] Be the credit of this Provincial Council, however, what it may, it is historically certain that, down to this date, no canon was received in the Western Church as a binding law for the payment of any defined portion of the annual increase of a man's substance—or Agobard, Bishop of Lyons, in whose province Mâcon was situated, would not have been able to state so confidently as he did many years afterward, that no decree had been settled in any Church synod, no decision had been publicly announced by the holy fathers, respecting contributions or the mode of distributing them. "For," says he, in explanation, "there was no need for such urgency when there was everywhere a glow of religious devotion, and a spontaneous desire to beautify the churches."[2]

It seems to have been somewhere about six hundred years after the death of Christ that an offering of some amount or other was made compulsory upon Christian disciples by excommunication. But the proportion was not even yet defined. The true Christian was described, in an exhortation written

---

[1] It is a singular fact, and tends to throw some discredit on this Council, that no compilation of synodal decrees published before the time of Charles V. mentions a single canon decreed thereat. Friar Crabbe, whose *Concilia Omnia, tam generalia quam particularia* first appeared in 1538, is the first who published the canon referred to in the text.

[2] Agobardus Lugdunensis de dispensatione Dei, p. 276, edit. Massoniana. Parisiis. His words are (4 cap. 20): "Jam vero de donandis rebus et ordinandis Ecclesiis, nihil unquam in Synodis constitutum est, nihil a sanctis patribus publice prædicatum. Nulla enim compulit necessitas, fervente ubique religiosa devotione et amore illustrandi Ecclesias ultro æstuante," &c.

about the eighth century, as one who "attends church frequently, tastes not of his own fruits until he has offered some portion of them to the Lord, pays tithes every year for the use of the poor, &c."[1] But no general law, of which we have any record, or to which the slightest historical credit can be given, ordained payment of tithes in the Western Church, until towards the beginning of the ninth century.[2] That there were special consecrations of tithes by *royal authority*, as early as A.D. 750, may be admitted — of which the grant, made by King Pepin, of the tithes of all that lay between the rivers Ourt and Lesche in Ardennes, to the church at S. Monon, is an illustration[3] — but they could not have been much in use — for amongst all the *formulæ* or precedents of deeds, conveyances, and grants, by which lands or profits were given to particular churches (of which we have a careful collection made by Marculphus, in the reign of Clovis II., about the middle of the seventh century), not a single instance occurs of a private conveyance or bequest of tithes.[4]

The groundwork of tithes, as a system of compulsory contributions to the Western Church, is to be found in the laws made by Charlemagne, in the eleventh year of his reign over France, Italy and Lombardy (A.D. 780)[5], and about twenty years after-

---

[1] MS. in Biblioth. Cotton, apud Selden, chap. v, sect. vi. p. 66.
[2] Selden, chap. v. sect. 6, at the end.
[3] Selden, chap. v. sect. 2.
[4] Ibid. at the end.
[5] The words are: "ut unusquisque suam Decimam donet; atque per jussionem Episcopi sui dispensetur." Cited by Selden, chap. vi. sect. 7.

ward incorporated in the laws of the empire. In a general assembly of estates, spiritual and temporal, convoked by the king at the first mentioned date, or thereabouts, it was ordained "That every one should pay his tithe." As illustrating the spirit of this law, it will be as well to look at one of the Constitutions of the same Charlemagne, levelled at such as would not give tithe unless it was purchased of them for a valuable consideration. This purchase was forbidden, "and if anyone shall be convicted of neglect" (to pay his tithe), "if he be *noster homo*" ("one in our service," we presume), "he shall be brought before us — but all others shall be distrained upon, that the unwilling may restore to the Church what they have neglected voluntarily to give."[1]

This Imperial law, taken together with the Imperial Constitution just quoted, may be regarded as the birth of the tithe system in the Western Church. Not much evidence here in support of the modern assumption that parochial tithes had their origin in individual and private liberality! Authority commanded and threatened to enforce what the emperor's subjects would not voluntarily give. Law was put into operation to supply the supposed defect of gospel motives. But even this expedient was not immediately successful. The law and the constitution too, remained little better than a dead letter

---

[1] Benedictus Levita, Capitular. lib. v. cap. 46: "De Decimas quas populus dare non vult, nisi quolibet modo ab eo redimantur; ab Episcopis prohibendum est ne fiat; et siquis contemplare inventus fuerit, si noster homo fuerit ad præsentiam nostram venire compellatur; cæteri vero destringantur ut inviti Ecclesiæ restituant quæ voluntarie dare neglexerunt."

for many years — "nothing being more frequent," as Selden tells us upon the highest historical authority, "than not only denying the clergy what they would have had, but also the taking from them what they otherwise possessed."[1]

[1] See Baronius and other authorities quoted by Selden, chap. vi. sect. 7, p. 132.

CHAP. III.

TITHES IN ENGLAND — THEIR ORIGIN IN LAW.

As in the Western Empire, so in England, the first authority for the payment of tithes was exclusively ecclesiastical — and as there, so here, that authority was recognised or rejected by every individual according as his conscience might receive or repudiate the doctrine, revere or despise the laws, of the Church. The devouter sort, no doubt, listened to exhortations on this head, and offered their tithes where they were believed to be due — the yet unchristianised, the irreligious, and the careless took no notice either of ecclesiastical constitutions nor of Church censures, and either wholly omitted, or very partially observed, the obligation so carefully enforced upon their consciences by the priesthood. We do not, therefore, deem it worth while to make further search than has been made already for the earliest canons promulgated on this head in this country. Indeed, they were very few, prior to the establishment of the tithe system by State authority, or, at any rate, very few have come down to us. The canon attributed to Egbert, Archbishop of York, and brother of Eadbert, King of Northumberland, dating about the middle of the eighth century[1], and the Decree of the General Council held for the whole kingdom at Calchuth[2] (wherever that may have been) A.D. 787, are the only proofs of the action of exclusively ecclesiastical authority in this matter which seem to have escaped the ravages of time.

As we approach the dawn of the ninth century, however, we light upon the first instance of a legal creation of tithe as a separate property for the maintenance of the clergy. Offa, King of Mercia, the most powerful of the Saxon kings in the English Heptarchy, was an esteemed friend and correspondent of Charlemagne.[3] His moral character, assuredly, was none of the best — for history lays to his charge the treacherous murder of Ethelbert, King of the East Angles, whom he had invited to his court to

---

[1] This canon is found in a collection of canons culled out of the ancient Fathers and Decrees of Councils. It bears the name of Egbert, but it is very doubtful whether it was drawn up by his hand, or under his authority. The reader who is curious on this point may consult Selden, chap. viii. sect. 1; Dr. Comber's "Book of Tithes," Part 1, chap. 8; Stillingfleet's "Treatise of the Duties of the Parochial Clergy," and Dean Prideaux's "Original and Right of Tithes," chap. iii. p. 93, ed. 1736. The canon is, unquestionably, an ancient one, and if the collection in which it is found be really Egbert's, and was designed as is said, to set forth the rules by which his province was to be ecclesiastically governed, it furnishes high authority for the tripartite division of tithes in England in the Saxon times; for it distinctly enacts that when the priests shall have received tithes from the people, and shall have had the names of those who have paid them written down, they shall, according to canonical authority, divide them in the presence of witnesses, one part to be for the ornamentation of the church, one for the use of poor and strangers, and the third part to be reserved for themselves. But, unquestionably, if this collection of canons be Egbert's, there are several interpolations in them by a later hand.

[2] This council was only an ecclesiastical synod, although held for the whole kingdom under the presidency of two cardinal legates from Rome.

[3] Matthew Paris, *in Vita Offæ secundi.*

marry his daughter.[1] Perhaps, it was to show him how so atrocious a crime might be best atoned for, that Charlemagne sent over to his red-handed brother a collection of synodical epistles and decrees, setting forth the principles of the Catholic faith, which imperial token of remembrance Offa is said to have received as if it had been " a gift from heaven."[2] Be this as it may, the Saxon king seems to have concluded that his readiest and surest method of purging himself of the blood he had spilt would be by following the example of the great emperor, and enriching the clergy at the expense of his subjects. So, in A.D. 794, instigated or assisted thereto by Theophilact, Bishop of Todi, one of the two legates sent over to England by Pope Hadrian I. with a view to reform and establish ecclesiastical laws in this island[3], he united with Kenulph, King of West Saxony, in summoning a council for the southern part of England, at which, we are told, all the nobles of the region, ecclesiastical and secular, gave attendance.[4] This council, or parliament, or State legis-

---

[1] Brompton Chronic. col. 754.

[2] Matthew Paris, ibid. What these synodical epistles and decrees were has been the subject of controversy; but it seems most probable that they included Charlemagne's Capitularies, in which the civil right of tithes is established.

[3] Pope Hadrian despatched two legates to England for this purpose, one to the court of Offa and one to that of Aelfwold. The particulars are related in a letter from those legates to the Pope. Gregory, Bishop of Ostia, visited Aelfwold. He seems to have sped so well with his mission, as to have been able to obtain civil as well as ecclesiastical recognition of all the decrees and canons he had proposed, and to have returned to the court of Offa, with ambassadors from Aelfwold, in time to be present at Offa's grand council. Mercland and Northumberland comprehended the best part of England. Selden, chap. viii. sect. 2.

[4] Of the council in Northumberland, the legates, in their letter to

lative authority of that day, passed a law which seems to have been accepted and passed a short time before by a similar council convened by Aelfwold, King of Northumberland.[1] The law of tithes after certain citations from Scripture, proceeds: "Wherefore, with obtestation, we enjoin that all be careful to pay tithes of all that they possess (because they are the special property of the Lord our God) and maintain themselves and give alms of the nine parts." But because the historical authority on which the foregoing account rests has been challenged, and because the law as thus established covered only a part, albeit the greater part of England, we hurry on to a somewhat later date, in quest of a broader legal foundation of the tithe system in this country.

It is now rather more than a thousand years ago that Ethelwolf, King of the West Saxons, on his return from Rome, whither he had been to pay his devotions, found his crown in considerable jeopardy.[2] During his absence, which was protracted above a twelvemonth, Aelstan, Bishop of Sherbourn, had contrived so to use his ecclesiastical influence, as to prevail on the nobility to form a party for deposing

the Pope, say: "ad diem consilii convenerunt omnes principes regionis, tam ecclesiastici quam seculares." The lay element of Offa's Council is not so distinctly exhibited.

[1] The constitutions or decrees passed in the Northumberland Council and brought with him thence by Gregory, Bishop of Ostia, were read through at the Mercian Council, chapter by chapter, as well in Latin as in Saxon, and were unanimously adopted.

[2] It seems, however, that Ethelwolf, as King of the West Saxons, had made a grant of tithes to the church, *for that kingdom*, before he set out for Rome, at Wilton, A.D. 854. William of Malmesbury and Matthew of Westminster have confounded this grant with the more general one, given under circumstances of much greater solemnity at Winchester.

the monarch, and placing his eldest son, Ethelbald, on his throne.[1] The king appears to have very sagaciously surmised that the wisest step he could take out of his difficulty, was to hold out a special inducement to the clergy to sustain his authority. What were the preliminaries we do not know. But history informs us that at a parliament convened at Winchester (A.D. 855) representing all England, and attended by the tributary kings, princes, bishops, and nobles of the land, after peace had been re-established between Ethelwolf and his son, a law of tithes for the whole realm of England was passed by general consent.[2] This law, as constituting the basis of the tithe system in England, we give entire.

"1. Our Lord Jesus Christ reigning for ever. Whereas, in our time we have seen the burnings of war, the ravagings of our wealth, and also the cruel depredations of enemies wasting our land, and many tribulations from barbarous and pagan nations inflicted upon us, for the punishing of our sins, even almost to our utter destruction, and also very perilous times hanging over our heads:[3] —

---

[1] See the chronicles of the times, in which the whole story is set forth.

[2] Ingulph, secretary to William I. in Normandy before the Conquest, and afterwards made Abbot of Croyland, in relating the circumstances attending the passing of this grant, thus describes the effect of it, showing the sense in which it had been understood up to his time,— "Then first he endowed the whole English Church with the tithes of all lands, and of other goods or chattels." p. 17.

[3] The reference, no doubt, is to the successive irruptions of the Danes, and to the miseries which his subjects had endured from the hands of these barbarous freebooters. But, perhaps, the last clause of the passage glances at the serious disaffection which had been fomented in his kingdom during his absence at Rome, and to the difficulties arising out of it not yet wholly subdued.

"2. For this cause, I, Ethelwulph, King of the West Saxons, by the advice of my bishops and other chief men of my kingdom, have resolved on a wholesome and uniform remedy — that is, that I grant as an offering unto God, and the Blessed Virgin, and all the Saints, a certain portion of my kingdom to be held by perpetual right, that is to say, the tenth part thereof[1]; and that this tenth part be privileged from temporal duties, and free from all secular services and royal tributes, as well the greater as the lesser, or those taxes which we call *Witerden*[2]; and that it be free from all things else, for the health of my soul and the pardon of my sins, to be applied only to the service of God alone, without being charged to any expedition, or to the repair of bridges, or the fortifying of castles, to the end that the clergy may, with the more diligence, pour out their prayers to God for us without ceasing, in which we do in some part receive their service.

"3. These things were enacted at Winchester, in the Church of St. Peter, before the great altar, in the year of the incarnation of our Lord 855, in the third indiction, on the nones of November, for the honour of the glorious Virgin and Mother of God,

[1] The translation in the text is adopted from Prideaux (chap. iv. p. 110), who has ingeniously pieced together the various readings of Ingulph and Matthew of Westminster. The copy of the grant handed down to us by Ingulph is perfectly unintelligible in this particular passage, and has plainly suffered from the ignorance of transcribers. The restoration by Prideaux appears legitimate, and certainly gives a sense in conformity with the view taken of the effect of the grant, not merely by Ingulph, but also by Asser, who lived in Ethelwolf's time; by Ethelwerd, a descendant of the king; by William of Malmesbury and other ancient chroniclers.

[2] Witerden, or Wynterden, or Witeredden,—for it is variously written —was a tax or royal aid, imposed by Saxon Parliaments.

St. Mary, and of St. Michael the Archangel, and of the blessed Peter, Prince of the Apostles, and also of our blessed father Pope Gregory, and of all the Saints.

"4. There were present and subscribing hereto all the archbishops and bishops of England, as also Boerred, King of Mercia, and Edmund, King of the East Angles, and also a great multitude of abbots, abbesses, dukes, earls, and noblemen, of the whole land, as well as of other Christian people, who all approved of the Royal Charter — but those only who were persons of dignity subscribed their names to it.

"5. King Ethelwulph, for the greater firmness of the grant, offered this Charter upon the altar of St. Peter the Apostle; and the bishops, on God's part, received the same of him, and afterwards sent it to be published in all the churches throughout their respective diocesses."

Here then, we have the foundation of the civil right of the clergy to tithes in England. We make no comment on the curiosities of this document. We cannot stay for that. It suffices us to note that it records, not the exercise of individual piety and liberality, but an enactment of public law.[1]

King Alfred, Ethelwolf's son, in a code of laws published during his reign for the better ordering of his realm, inserted in it a law for the rendering of

---

[1] It is true this law differs in form and style very materially from our modern Acts of Parliament. But it is quite in accordance with the usage of the then times. That it was not a mere personal act of royalty is clear from the subscription thereto of the lay nobles of the realm.

tithes to God[1]—and in the league he made with Guthrun, King of the Danes[2], wherein he ceded to him, after the Danish monarch's conversion to Christianity, the provinces of Northumberland and East Anglia, he set forth certain laws to be observed, amongst which is to be found the following:—" That if any man shall withhold his tithes, and not faithfully and duly pay them to the Church, if he be a Dane he shall be fined in the sum of twenty shillings, and if an Englishman, in the sum of thirty shillings."[3] This law was renewed and confirmed between Guthrun and Edward, Alfred's son, during Alfred's lifetime.

The next law (in order of time) for the universal payment of tithes in this kingdom, was made about A.D. 924 by King Athelstan — and it is worthy of notice for two reasons.[4] First because it recited *as*

---

[1] The words are " Decimas primigenia, et adulta tua Deo dato."

[2] Guthrun, King of the Danes, on his conversion to Christianity, entered into treaty with Alfred, who ceded to him the provinces of East Anglia and Northumberland *en suzerainté*. The code of laws referred to in the text may be regarded as treaty stipulations.

[3] The words as translated into Latin were, " Si quis Decimam contrateneat, reddat *Lashlite* cum Dacis, *Witam* cum Anglis." *Lashlite* denoted a common forfeiture among the Danes, amounting to twelve *Ores*, which, at the usual rate of about twenty pence to the *Ore*, make twenty shillings. *Witam* was the common fine among the English, namely, thirty shillings.

[4] This law is worth transcription for curiosity sake. We translate it that the English reader may have the full benefit of its reasoning:

" I, Athelstan, King, by the advice of Wolfhelm, my Archbishop, and of my other Bishops, command and enjoin all my Sheriffs, in the name of the Lord and of all the Saints, and as they tender my favour, to pay out of my proper substance to God, tithes, as well of cattle as of the fruits of the earth. And let all my Bishops do the same out of their proper substance, and my Earls and my Sheriffs. And I will that my Bishops and Sheriffs administer justice in this matter to all over whom they have jurisdiction. And let them complete this business by the day *a portion of Scripture* the following sentence, which it would puzzle all the bishops to discover therein:—" If we will not pay our tithes, the tenth part only shall be left us, and the other nine shall be taken from us "— and secondly, because it contains the first legal mention we have of Church-scot (a certain portion of corn paid to the clergy out of the first threshing after the harvest). The clause is in these words:—" I will that the Church-scot[1] be paid to that place to which it doth belong, that there they may enjoy them who by their ministerial service shall best deserve them from God and us."

In A.D. 944, Edmund, brother of Athelstan, and his successor to the throne made a law for the payment of tithe, Church-scot, and plough-alms, or Peter's pence.[2]

---

we have fixed, namely, the feast of the beheading of John the Baptist. Let us reflect upon what Jacob said to God, 'I will offer unto Thee tithes and peace offerings.' And the Lord hath said in the Gospel 'to him that hath shall be given, and he shall abound.' We are also to recollect how terribly it is laid down in the same book, 'If we are unwilling to pay tenths, that the nine parts shall be taken from us, and only a tenth shall be left.' And I will that Church-scot be paid to that place to which it doth belong, so that they may rejoice in it who, by their service of God and us, are most worthy of it. The Divine word exhorts us to win eternal by earthly things, and things that are heavenly by things that fade away." Spelm. Concil. i. p. 396. How like a law prompted by episcopal wisdom!

[1] As this is the first law in which Church-scot is introduced, it may be as well to correct the modern notion which confounds it with Church-rate, by giving Selden's learned explanation of it. He tells us that *Cyryscrat*, sometimes written *Curescet*, and in Doomsday Book *Circset*, is a church rent of corn, or the first fruits of corn yearly of those times, and regularly payable at St. Martin's day to the Church, in the time of the ancient Britons, as well as of the Saxons. It was really first-fruits, and was so called after the introduction of the Normans. It differed as much from Church-rate as that differs from tithes.

[2] " Decimas præcipimus omni Christiano super Christianitatem suam

His son, King Edgar, in A.D. 967, followed in the steps of his royal ancestors. His law contains the following highly coercive provision:—" And if any one shall refuse to pay his tithes in such manner as we have prescribed, then let the king's sheriff, and the bishop of the diocese, and the minister of the parish come together, and let them *by force* cause the tenth part to be paid to the church to which it was due, leaving only the ninth part to the owner. And for the other eight parts, the lord of the manor shall have one four parts, and the bishop of the diocese the other four."[1] A curious illustration this of spontaneous and private liberality in endowing the Church with parochial tithes!

Ethelred, son of Edgar, contributed two laws to the foregoing—one in A.D. 1008, and a second in A.D. 1012, both of which were agreed to by the parliament of the day. The last of these we may as well quote:—" We command that every man, for the love of God and all the saints, shall pay his Church-scot and his full tithe, in the same manner as it was done in those times of our predecessors when it was best done—that is that he pay for tithe every tenth

dare." See Spelman Concil. vol. i. p. 420. Plough-alms, or alms-money, Selden tells us, was the Peter pence due yearly on the 31st of August, on the institution, as some say of King Ina, as others of King Ethelwolf.

[1] Edgar's law, which is inserted at length in the Brompton Chronicle, is remarkable, not merely on account of its highly coercive provisions, but also because he was the first of the Saxon kings who directed payment of tithes to the mother Church. The words of the first clause are " Primum est, ut Ecclesiæ Dei recti sui dignæ sint, et reddatur omnis Decimatio *ad matrem Ecclesiam cui Parochia adjacet*, de terra Thainorum et villanorum, sicut aratrum peragrabit." The second clause, which deserves to be noted, will have to be considered when we come to discuss the arbitrary disposition of tithes.

acre that the plough shall go over. And every other customary due must be paid to the Mother Church to which every man belongs for the love of God. And let no man take from God what belongs to God, and which our predecessors have consecrated to him."[1]

Canute, in a parliament held at Westminster A.D. 1032, revived and re-enacted, with additional penalties, the law of Edgar for tithes, plough-alms, and Church-scot.[2]

After the conquest of England by William of Normandy, he called a parliament composed of twelve men chosen from each county to ascertain the laws by which the kingdom had been governed in the reign of Edward the Confessor—and the laws thus ascertained, constituting the foundation of what is called "the common law" of England, he re-enacted. Amongst them is one for payment of tithe which we quote, so far at least as it bears on our present object of inquiry. "Of all corn the tenth sheaf is due to God, and therefore is to be paid unto him. If any one shall have a herd of mares, let him pay the tenth colt, but if he have only one or two mares, let him pay a penny for every colt which he shall have of them. In like manner if he shall have many cows, he shall pay the tenth calf; if he shall have

---

[1] Brompton Chron. col. 902.

[2] Ibid., col. 920. Besides tithes and Church-scot, Canute enacts "Thrice every year a certain sum of money must be paid for the maintaining of lights (wax-candles) at the parish church, that is to say, for every hide of land a halfpenny at Easter, another halfpenny at the solemn festival of All Saints, and the like at the festival of the purification of St. Mary. And it is fitting that at the digging of every grave the burial fee should forthwith be paid to the priest."

but one or two cows, then he shall pay a halfpenny for every calf. And he who shall make cheese must give unto God the tenth cheese; but he that shall make none must give the milk of every tenth day. And so likewise must be paid the tenth lamb, the tenth fleece, the tenth part of the butter, and the tenth pig. And so, in like manner, of the bees, the tenth part of the profit. And so likewise of woods, of meadows, of waters and mills, of parks, of ponds, of fisheries, of copse, of orchards and gardens, and *of trade*, and of all things which the Lord shall give, the tenth part is to be rendered to Him who giveth unto us the other nine parts with that tenth. Whosoever shall withhold this tenth part shall, by the justice of the bishop and the king, be forced to the payment of it, if need be."[1]

Henry I.[2], Stephen[3], and Henry II.[4], were obliged to swear to the maintenance and observance of the laws collected and published by Edward the Confessor. But having brought down this review to close upon the beginning of the thirteenth century, it will be needless to weary the reader with further repetitions. The fact that we have on record such a continuous succession of laws for the payment of parochial tithes for a period of about four hundred

[1] Hoveden's Annals Pars. Post, p. 602. Spelman, Concil. vol. i. p. 620.
[2] Matthew Paris (or rather Roger of Wendover) under the year A.D. 1100.
[3] The Charter of Stephen, confirming the laws of Edward the Confessor, is extant in the Red Book in the Exchequer, and is quoted by Coke in the Preface to the 8th part of his Reports.
[4] Brady's Appendix to the first volume of his History of England, No. 40, p. 40.

years of the earlier history of our country, is utterly inexplicable on the hypothesis of the tithe endowment system having had its origin in the spontaneous liberality of individuals. This fact, however, fatal as it is to any such hypothesis, is not, by any means, the strongest of the arguments to be adduced against it. But it does constitute a very respectable groundwork for the conclusion we are seeking to establish —namely, that the public law of England, and not the private liberality of individuals, created the tithe system, as a provision for the maintenance of the clergy of this country.

CHAP. IV.

LAY RECUSANCY IN REGARD TO TITHES.

THE period within which the tithe system was originally planted and took root in England ranges between the closing years of the Heptarchy and the signing of Magna Charta. Within those limits will be found the beginnings of it, whether it sprang out of individual liberality, or of public law. We have glanced at what civil authority did during those four centuries to give effect to the wishes of ecclesiastics in this matter. We have now to trace the effect of legislation on the people at large. We shall collect from the most authentic sources such evidence as exists of the kind of spontaneity which our "pious forefathers" are said by some of their admiring posterity to have exemplified in their endowment of parish churches. It will be found, we think, very greatly to resemble the readiness of parishioners in these days to pay church-rates — when they are obliged to do it.

We direct attention, first of all, to the general characteristics and condition of the people of England throughout those times. Persons are apt to delude themselves with a dreamy sort of notion that, during the period to which we refer, England, at least in a

Roman Catholic sense, was pre-eminently Christian. But nothing is more contrary to fact, regard being had to the population generally. On the contrary, one inundation of heathenism swept over the land so closely after another, as to render it morally impossible that the people should have become either widely or deeply imbued with Christian doctrine. The Roman Church, it is true, rapidly subjugated the rude courts of both Saxon and Danish princes, and, with them, the higher nobility — but her influence could only have slowly descended from the summits to the level plains of society. Scarcely had the Saxon kings given heed to episcopal teaching when Danish invasions troubled the eastern provinces, and for upwards of a hundred and fifty years, with an alternate flow and ebb of fortune, advanced steadily towards the west.[1] A very short time after these irruptions ceased, William of Normandy conquered the whole kingdom. Through the six or eight generations among whom the germs of the tithe system were planted, the scanty population of this island, unequally divided between a miserable peasantry and a ferocious aristocracy, and living, the one in squalid cabins and in uncleared woods, the other in frowning castles surrounded by poorly cultivated estates, could have been, for the most part, Christian in name only — often, and in large tracts of country, not even

---

[1] "From the time of King Ethelwolf, who first made the grant of tithes, to the last renewal of it by King Canute, the kingdom underwent terrible convulsions by reason of the Danish war, which miserably harassed the land for full two hundred years, and oftentimes a great part and sometimes in a manner the whole of it, was in the enemy's hands." Prideaux's "Original and Right of Tithes," chap. iv.

that.[1] It can easily be understood how, at a time when three-fourths of England, at least, were as wild and waste as modern States in the far west of America, and when the few bishops were chief statesmen in the courts of England's kings, large grants of yet unappropriated land were given, and stringent laws for the payment of tithes to the clergy were enacted, without implying any large amount of Christian liberality among the people generally.[2] It is not among tribes dimly conscious of any religious restraints, prone to the indulgence of the grossest appetites, the whole history of whom is but a history of wrongs inflicted upon one another, that one can rationally look for that general liberality, which the universal endowment of our parish churches by private donations or bequests necessarily presupposes.

Nor is it easy to account for such a long succession of laws for tithe, if the disposition to give tithe spontaneously were a characteristic of the age. Almost every monarch, on his accession to the throne, or within a year or two of it, summoned around him his nobles and bishops, and solemnly promulgated a new law for the payment of tithes to the church. Offa and Aelfwold, Ethelwolf, Alfred, Athelstan, Edmund, Edgar, Canute, Edward the Confessor, William the Conqueror, Henry I., Stephen, Henry II. —how came it to be necessary that each of them should re-enact or confirm the tithe system, if within

---

[1] See Macaulay's "History of England," chap. i. pp. 8, 9, 10.

[2] It deserves to be noted here that the most important of our ecclesiastical structures were erected *after* the Norman Conquest.

their time individual beneficence and piety had been so common as to cover the land with what is called "lay foundations?" Dean Prideaux tells us that the law was thus repeated in each reign partly because the Danish troubles made it necessary, and partly on account of its supreme excellence—and he finds a parallel in the case of Magna Charta, which Coke tells us was re-enacted or confirmed above thirty times.[1] But the parallel only strengthens our case. For Magna Charta was meant to bind the sovereign, and it was because successive sovereigns resented, or were suspected of resenting, that restraint, that it was thought necessary to bind them again and again. Who ever heard of the same law, in substance, being repeated, reign after reign, for a period of between three and four hundred years, except it were so far disregarded, as to render this re-declaration of royal and parliamentary authority a matter of necessity?

The point we are aiming to bring out may be further illustrated by evidence of the gradual but ever progressive enlargement of ecclesiastical demands. The clergy felt their way, cautiously at first, but ever as they made good their ground they insisted upon more. On the continent, it is certain that, in the earlier times of the tithe system, there was

---

[1] The words of Coke, quoted from the Preface to the 8th part of his Reports, are "The Great Charters made by King John do, in effect, agree with Magna Charta and Charta de Foresta, established and confirmed by the Great Charter made in the ninth of King Henry III., which for their excellency have since that time been confirmed, and commanded to be put in execution by the wisdom and authority of thirty several Parliaments and above."

a quadripartite distribution of tithes; one part being assigned to the bishop, one to the ministering clergyman, one to the repair of the church, and one to the relief of the poor. In this kingdom, however, such a distribution of tithe seems to have soon fallen into disuse. Among the canons attributed to Egbert, Archbishop of York, about the middle of the eighth century, prior canonical authority is alleged, and enforced, for a tripartite division of tithes " before witnesses "—one for the decoration of the church, one for the use of the poor and strangers, and a third part for the ministering clergyman.[1] And this Canon of Egbert is found in a collection of Synodical Statutes made about the time of King Athelstan. We can discover no other authority for a tripartite distribution of tithes in England—but that which we have already cited indicates that Augustine, when he laid the foundation of the Roman Church in this island, acted upon the advice tendered him, in answer to his own inquiries, by Pope Gregory.[2]

If this division of tithes really were the original practice in England, as Blackstone tells us it was, the clergy soon found means to get rid of it, and to

[1] See chap. iii. note 1.
[2] Augustine writes to Pope Gregory to inquire how the oblations which the faithful bring to the altar are to be divided. The Pope replies that it is usual with the apostolical see at the ordination of bishops to charge them to divide the whole income into four parts, one for the bishop and his family, that he may be able to practise hospitality; one for the clergy; one for the poor, and one for the repair of churches. But he adds an admonition that, out of tenderness to the Anglo-Saxon Church, he and his clergy should still imitate the community of goods used in the primitive times under the Apostles. Bede's " Eccles. Hist." lib. iii. cap. 23; Selden, chap. ix. sect. 2.

appropriate the whole to their own use.[1] Even this, however, did not content them. Before A.D 940, they had set up and established a claim to Church-scot and alms money. Their original demand for tithes of the earth's fruits, soon widened to take in cattle—then extended to milk, cheese, and wool—seeds, fruit, mast, and honey—pigeons, rabbits, fish, and deer—the proceeds of hawking, hunting, fishing (for sport), and fowling—the profits of mills, stone and slate quarries—the sale of copse-wood and timber—and the earnings of merchants, traders, artificers, handicraftsmen, and labourers of every description. The claims of the clergy on several of these items were resisted by the laity as soon as they were made—some of them successfully. During the reigns of Edward III., Richard II., and Henry IV., complaint after complaint was made by the Commons to the Crown against the encroachments of the ecclesiastical order, and praying that they might be stayed by prohibition.[2] Indeed, in every parish, custom

[1] Blackstone's "Commentaries," bk. i. chap. xi. sect. v.

[2] The Commons of those days usually made their complaints against the encroachments of the ecclesiastical order in the shape of a petition or address to the Crown. In the 17th year of Edward III.'s reign, the Commons pray in Norman-French that "No man may be pursued in Courts Christian for tithes of timber or underwood, except in places where such tithes had been customarily paid." To which the answer of the Crown was; "Be it done in this matter as it has been done up to this time." The clergy, however, seem to have persisted in their novel exactions. Petitions went up against them from the Commons in the 18th, the 21st, and the 25th years of Edward III., and at length in the 45th year of that reign, on a petition of the Lords Temporal and the Commons it was enacted that timber of above twenty years' growth should be tithe free. A similar contest between Parliament and Convocation arose in Henry IV.'s time in reference to the tithing of quarries of stone and slate. Particulars may be found in most of the law books on the subject.

and usage were at length admitted, within certain limits, to be the authoritative interpreters of the law — and this was afterwards recognised and confirmed by 27 Hen. VIII. cap. 20, and 32 Hen. VIII. cap. 7.[1]

Well now, we put it to every candid and thoughtful person to state what is the impression left upon his mind by this summary of historical facts. Is it not, from beginning to end, utterly irreconcileable with the hypothesis that parochial tithes in this country had their origin in the spontaneous and pious beneficence of individual land proprietors? Is it intelligible on any other supposition than that of general law, first suggested by the doctrine of ecclesiastics, and enforced upon the conscience by Church censures, afterwards adopted by the Civil Power, and carried into effect by the aid of severe penalties, upon unwilling subjects? We have authority on the one hand, and disregard of it on the other — encroachments, in claim, met by resistance, in practice — disobedience menaced with increasingly ruinous punishments — struggles between clergy and laity generally ending in the triumph of the former — complaints, remonstrances, and confusion without end. If ever history read out its own moral, surely this does. It proves that the tithe system is not the final outcome of spontaneous piety, far less of indi-

[1] The 27 Hen. VIII. cap. 20, enacts that every one, " according to the ecclesiastical laws and ordinance of this Church of England, *and after the laudable usages and customs of the parish* or other place where he dwelleth or occupieth, shall yield and pay his tithes," &c. The 32 Hen. VIII. cap. 7, enjoins every man " fully, truly, and effectually to divide, set out, yield or pay all and singular tithes and offerings, *according to the lawful customs and usages* of the parishes and places where such tithes or duties shall grow, arise, come or be due."

vidual zeal, nor the rich and indigenous growth of lay devotion in earlier times, but is the precipitate of public law applied again and again, with ever increasing severity, to reluctant wills, and by its coercive and uniform action forcing out every where similar results. This will become still clearer, the further our researches are pushed.

But, indeed, we are not left to inference only — we have positive contemporaneous evidence that law *was* necessary to enforce payment of tithe. Thus when Athelstan had promulgated his law, he received an address of thanks from Kent, in which bishops, thanes, knights, and the common people, confessed there was "great need of it both for rich and poor."[1] And even so late as the reign of Edward I. we find a preamble of one of the chief English Canon Laws, in support of tithes, running thus : "Whereas, on account of the different customs of tithing prevalent in different churches, strifes, contentions, and the most abominable scandals are constantly arising between rectors of churches and their parishioners, we ordain,

---

[1] Bromptoni Chron. col. 850. The address was plainly enough drawn up by ecclesiastics. It is too enthusiastically grateful for lay conception. It indicates marvellous joy on the part of all classes, at the re-imposition of a law compelling them to do what they professed a desire, and a voluntary and grateful eagerness to do. Nevertheless, the confession slips out that the coercion of law had become very necessary. We give it as we find it. "Carissime! Episcopi tui de Kent, et omnis Kentsiræ, Thayni, Comites et villani, tibi Domino dulcissimo suo gratias agunt, quod nobis de pace nostra præcipere voluisti, et de commodo nostro perquirere et consulere, *quia magnum opus est inde nobis, divitibus et egenis.* Et hoc incepimus, quantâ diligentiâ potuimus, consilio horum sapientum quos ad nos misisti. Unde, Carissime Domine, *primum est de nostra Decima,* ad quam valdè cupidi sumus, et voluntarii, et tibi supplices gratias agimus admonitionis tuæ."

&c."[1] So, it is noted among the laws attributed to Edward the Confessor, that payment of tithes was much diminished. "But since then" (these are the words) "*by the instigation of the devil*, many have withheld their tithes, and priests, enriched from other sources, do not care to undergo the *trouble* of collecting them."[2] Coming down to the time of Edward III. and Richard II. we may cite Chaucer (in the "Ploughman's Tale") as illustrating the spirit of the age:—

> "Their tithing and their offering both,
> They clemeth it by possession;
> Thereof nil they none forego.
> But robben men by ransome."

And of rectors of parishes he writes thus:—

> "For the tithing of a ducke,
> Or an apple, or an aye[3],
> They make men swere upon a boke,
> Thus they foulen Christ's fay."[4]

But we have still more cogent proof of indisposition on the part of the laity to obey the laws relating to tithes, in the steadily increasing severity of the penalties imposed on the disobedient. In the laws of Offa, Aelfwold, and Ethelwolf, we have a mere recognition of the ecclesiastical claim by the Civil Power. In Ethelwolf's case, he gave greater solemnity to this recognition — this commutation of

---

[1] This is the preamble of the canon law made for tithes, prædial and personal, by a council held at London in the 23rd year of Edward I., under the presidency of Robert Winchelsea, Archbishop of Canterbury.

[2] Sed postea, *instinctû diaboli, multi Decimam detinuerunt*," &c. But Selden suspects that this addition to the law has been made by a somewhat later hand. "Hist. of Tithes," chap. x. sect. 2.

[3] Egg.   [4] Faith.

the demand of the Church, into a law of the State—by offering the document by which it was carried into effect upon the altar, and so, as it were, consecrating the act by religious sanctions. In the laws of Alfred we meet with the first instance of civil penalty adjudged for withholding tithe—namely, a fine of twenty shillings, if the offender were a Dane, and of thirty shillings, if he were an Englishman. But the threatened punishment does not appear to have been very effectual, in spite of its having been supplemented by ecclesiastical excommunications. Else, why do we find Edgar resorting to a far more stringent remedy, and assigning of the ten parts of every recusant's annual profits, four parts to the lord of the manor, and four to the bishop, leaving him but a tenth for his own subsistence?[1] That this severe penalty, although subsequently re-imposed by Canute[2] and Henry I.[3], did not wholly subdue the

[1] Bromptoni Chron. col. 871. "Si quis Decimam dare, sicut diximus, noluerit, adeant, Præpositus Regis, et Episcopus et Sacerdos illius Ecclesiæ, et reddant Ecclesiæ cui pertenebit Decimam suam; et nonam partem demittant ei qui Decimam suam detinuit, et octo partes in duo dividantur. Dimidium domino; dimidium episcopo — sit homo Regis, sit homo Thaini." If any penalty was likely to be enforced this was. The lord of the manor and the bishop of the diocese were equally interested in it to see to its execution. Yet, it does not seem to have been thoroughly effectual, or why should it have been renewed?

[2] Canute adopts very nearly the words of Edgar's law. He was thoroughly in earnest. Writing to his Bishops and nobles from Rome, whither, according to usage, he went to pay his devotion, he charges them to take effectual care that all dues to the church be enforced, and he concludes: "If, when I shall return, these and other dues remain unpaid, my royal prerogative shall be put in force, in accordance with the laws, against every defaulter, strictly and without mercy. See William of Malmesbury De Gestis Regum, lib. ii. cap. 11.

[3] Selden (chap. viii. sect. 17) quotes to this effect from a collection of the laws of Henry I. in the Red Book of the Exchequer, under the general heading "De placitis Ecclesiæ pertinentibus ad Regem."

recalcitrant laity, is clear enough, we think, from Pontifical and Synodal Decrees subsequently promulgated by the Church. Thus in the reign of Stephen "whoever is unwilling to pay tithes of his yearly increase, let sentence of anathema be passed upon him." In like manner, at a Provincial Synod for Canterbury, held at Westminster, the following was adopted :—"But, inasmuch as *many are now found unwilling to pay tithe*, we ordain that according to the precepts of the Lord the Pope, they be admonished a first, second, and third time—and if, being so admonished they shall not amend, let them know that they put themselves under anathema."[1]

---

[1] Hoveden's Annals, part 2, fol. 311. The words are " Omnes Decimæ terræ, sive de frugibus, sive de fructibus, Domini sunt, et illi sanctificantur. Sed quia multi modo inveniuntur Decimas dare nolentes, statuimus, ut juxta Domini Papæ præcepta, admoneantur semel, secundò, et tertiò, ut de grano, de vino, de fructibus arborum, de fœtibus animalium, de lana, de agnis, de butyro et caseo, de lino et canabe, et de reliquis quæ annuatim renovantur, Decimas in ægrè persolvant; quod si, commoniti, non emendaverint, anathemati se noverint subjacere." The synod referred to was held in the 21st year of the reign of Henry II.

CHAP. V.

THINGS LEGALLY TITHEABLE.

WE turn now to a totally different branch of the argument. We have done for the present with Anglo-Saxon and Norman laws. We propose, by way of change, to "take our walks abroad," and look over the rather ample catalogue of "things titheable," and of the customary and legal modes of "setting them out" for the use of the recipient. Possibly, we may pick up in this field several incidental confirmations of our main position, that tithe property could not have originated in the private liberality of manorial lords, but has its roots exclusively in public law — confirmations, however, which are only the stronger for being incidental. We will run over the list as cursorily as possible, noting by the way, the principles of law laid down in various instances, so far at least as they serve to strengthen our position, and reserving to the close any general observations which the survey may have suggested to us.

We begin the investigation with *prædial* tithes — so called because tithes of things *springing out of the earth*. These were divided into *great* and *small*. With a view to distinctness, and that the reader's memory, in dealing with such a multiplicity of details, may be assisted by the eye, we shall separate the information we think well to lay before him, into detached portions corresponding with the ordinary divisions of the law books.[1]

PRÆDIAL TITHES — GREAT.

1. These comprised, in the first place, *corn and grain*, under which denomination we are to include wheat[2], rye[3], barley, oats[4]; all sorts of pulse, such as pease[5] and beans[6], and tares or vetches.[7] We shall not trouble the reader with endless particulars, in which the legal courts have from time to time decided what were the rights of the farmer, and what the rights of the tithe-owner, in regard to the time at which, and the manner in which, tithes of these several crops were to be paid. But we note a general principle of law applicable to the whole of this class of " things titheable "—namely, that severance of the crop from the ground gave the tithe-

---

[1] We may as well save the reader the trouble of frequent reference, by stating that the law authorities we have followed throughout this chapter, are Sir Simon Degge's "Parson's Counsellor," and Eagle's "Law of Tithes."

[2] The common law mode of tithing wheat was in the sheaf, and not in the shock; the farmer being bound to bind up the parson's tenth in sheaf and to leave it a reasonable time in this state to be viewed, before proceeding to put the crop in shocks. But custom sanctioned a deviation from this established mode.

[3] Rye was tithed in like manner as wheat.

[4] Barley and oats were titheable by the heap or cock, except where it was the custom of the district to bind them in sheaves.

[5] No definite mode of setting out the tithe of pease is laid down in the law books.

[6] Beans were usually tithed in the sheaf or shock.

[7] Tares or vetches being usually cut down green, and used as food for cattle, were considered as in the nature of agistment.

owner his first right in his portion of the produce, and imposed upon the farmer his first duty in regard to it—no claim for tithe arising until the crop was severed, and no liberty to remove the crop being enjoyed until the tenth part of it could be conveniently separated and distinguished in such manner as to be fairly compared with the nine parts. That it devolved upon the farmer, in all cases, to furnish the labour necessary to gather in the whole ten parts of the harvest, and to separate the parson's tenth part from his own nine, we may point out as the first indication that *law*, and not individual goodwill, had constituted tithes a property.

2. The next article we have to mention under this head is *hay*—comprehending all the grasses, herbs, and vegetable products, when they were mown and dried for food for cattle. Three questions have arisen in regard to this kind of produce, the legal settlement of which illustrates our point. In the first place, the common law, as interpreted by the latest decisions, required the farmer not merely to cut down the grass for the tithe-owner, but to carry it through its first process of "tedding," before he made it into cocks for the purpose of tithe-viewing—a departure from the *general rule of law*, that the occupier is not obliged to do any act towards bettering the condition of the tithe for the benefit of the tithe-owner.[1] In the second place, another *general*

---

[1] The law courts held tithe to be a tenth part of the produce of the ground, and not of the labour and industry of the husbandman; but they also decided that things were not to be tithed before they were in a proper state to be tithed. However, by special custom, the parson

rule is departed from in respect of these crops—for whereas, the principle is laid down that "of all things that are renewed in the year tithes are due at once, and but once," in the case of hay the aftermath or second crop was titheable.[1] In the third place, grasses cut green and used in that state as food for cattle, have been decided to be an agistment tithe (which we shall presently explain) on the ground of another *principle of law* governing tithe practice—namely, that the tithe-owner cannot control the farmer in his mode of husbandry, provided he act *bonâ fide*, and without fraud.

3. We come next to the tithing of *wood*.[2] This is a comparatively modern subject of tithe law. It was never reckoned among titheable things by the Anglo-Saxons. As a portion of tithe property it had its origin in ecclesiastical law about A.D. 1305—was strenuously resisted by the laity from the first

might claim to have his tithe grass made into perfect hay without giving any recompense to the farmer.

[1] Tithe of after-math is supposed to have been sanctioned by law to prevent any fraud which might be attempted against the parson, by not mowing the first crop close enough to the ground.

[2] The first ecclesiastical law which makes mention of tithes of wood, is the constitution of Archbishop Winchelsea, at Merton, A.D. 1305, and the tithe made payable by that canon was probably only a personal tithe of the annual profits made by the sale of the article. It was first claimed as a præidal tithe by a canon made in a convocation of the clergy, under Archbishop Stratford, A.D. 1343, in the 17th year of Edward III. But this canon was never recognised by the law; it was stoutly resisted by parliament, and it was only after a long fight that the clergy gained, by a sort of compromise, an implied right to tithe underwood, timber trees of twenty years' growth and upwards being expressly excepted by statute law, as mentioned in the text. The contest from beginning to end is a curious and most instructive illustration of the mode in which the clergy of those times encroached on the rights and property of the laity, and how little they relied on voluntary and private liberality for their revenue.

—and was settled by the statute 45 Edward III. cap. 3[1], by a compromise to the effect that tithes should be payable of all wood except timber trees of the growth of twenty years and upwards, which is interpreted to include " their lops and tops "— and stems from their stumps after having been cut down. The *principle of law* on which the whole question of tithe in wood turned, was that timber trees are a parcel of the inheritance—nay, an inheritance in themselves — and are therefore exempted under the general rule that tithes are not to be paid of the inheritance, but only of the fruits of the inheritance; a principle illustrated by the case of copper, lead, and coal mines, and other things which are of *the substance* of the earth. We need not, however, dwell upon this item of titheable produce. No one will pretend that it ever was included in the category of tithes, but by a pure process of comparatively modern law.

PRÆDIAL TITHES — SMALL.

1. *Agistment*, to which we give precedence in the rank of " small " tithes, was the tithe of grass or herbage eaten by cattle at pasture.[2] It was payable,

---

[1] The act of the 45 Edw. III. cap. 3, in consequence of a pretence raised by the clergy that it was not duly passed, was confirmed by another statute passed in the next parliament, in 47 Edw. III., and afterwards by two statutes, in 8 Rich. II. and 9 Hen. VI.

[2] The word *agistment* which signifies the feeding and depasturing of cattle, is said, in the law books, to be derived from the French word *agiser*; because, in those places where cattle are taken to be fed for hire, the cattle are suffered *agiser*, that is, to be *levant* and *couchant* there. Whatever species of titheable produce is severed from the ground by the mouth of an animal comes under the denomination of *agistment*.

by common right, for the depasturing of barren and unprofitable cattle only, not of profitable animals, such as milch cows and sheep, which, in another shape, benefited the tithe-owner, who could claim his tenth on calves, milk, lambs, and wool.[1] For the same reason, this kind of tithe was not due on horses and oxen used in the husbandry of the farm, because the parson drew a profit from their labour in maturing tithe produce—nor on young cattle reared for the plough or pail[2]—nor on pleasure horses which yielded no gains to the farmer[3]—nor on animals *feræ naturæ*, such as deer and rabbits—nor on cattle which had trespassed or strayed upon the farm. All these exemptions, it will be seen, had their origin in the *principle of common law*, that tithe was a tenth part of *profits* annually arising, and that it was not payable on what was necessary to produce those profits. But, indeed, all the minute rules laid down by law, to govern the payment of this kind of tithe, point, distinctly enough, to its legal origin, and help to dissipate the notion that this species of property

---

[1] But this exemption of profitable cattle only applied in cases where they were profitable to the parson of the parish in which they were agisted, as well as to the farmer. For instance, if cattle which were employed in husbandry in one parish were depastured in another where they were not so employed, they paid tithes of agistment to the parson of the latter parish, because he derived no benefit from their labour.

[2] Unless their destination were altered, and they were sold out of the parish before they had become profitable, in which case they were subject to tithes for their depasturage.

[3] Saddle horses were exempt, except where special custom to the contrary determined otherwise; but an innkeeper was liable for horses of travellers, or for those of his own which were kept for hire, depastured on his land.

2. This conclusion becomes clearer when we step from the fields to the orchard and the garden — where we meet with *fruit, garden herbs, roots, and vegetables,* as " titheable produce." Of these, comprehending apples (whether gathered or windfalls), pears, plums, cherries, (including wild cherries growing in hedge rows), peaches, nectarines, apricots, grapes, gooseberries, currants, raspberries, strawberries, walnuts, and other fruits; mint, sage, rue, parsley, celery, cabbages, cauliflowers, carrots, parsnips, onions, radishes, and cucumbers—several sorts (not to say full one half) were unknown to the " pious ancestors " who are assumed to have set apart a tenth of them, both such as they grew themselves, and such as their tenants and serfs grew, " to God and the Church " to all future generations.[2] It would, no doubt, have been abundantly liberal in them thus to dispose of a portion of " garden stuff " to be raised within the circuit of their estates, by every poor cottager who might cultivate a little patch of soil therein, a thousand years after they themselves

---

[1] Take, for example, agistment of after-pasture, In this case, the common law had over and over again decided that the feeding of barren and unprofitable cattle on meadows or arable land from which hay or corn had been mowed or reaped, and for which tithes had been paid in the same year, did not subject them to tithe of agistment, on the ground that " the parson shall not have a double tithe of one and the same thing in one year." The clergy, however, as usual in those days, were persistent in their claim, and were only foiled at last, by a declaratory act of parliament passed in the 2nd year of Henry IV.

[2] Fruits and plants raised in hot-houses and green-houses, do not seem to have been subject to a demand for tithe previously to the year 1781.

had slept their last sleep—but we must persist in the liberty of asserting that they either gave away what was not theirs to bestow, or that they were not so absurdly presumptuous as some of their modern posterity would have us suppose—in a word, that, in addition to the fact that many of these productions have been introduced to England since their time, the all-comprehensiveness, the uniformity, and the permanency of this tax-in-kind upon rich and poor, lord and tenant, franklin and villain, prove conclusively enough that it could have had its origin in *public law* only.

3. Turning back from the garden to the fields again, we cast our eyes upon *turnips* and *potatoes*, grown as field crops. These, it is well known, were brought to England centuries after the age when the tithe-system was established—the last-mentioned since the passing of the statute 2 and 3 Edward VI. cap. 13. The law, however, laid hold on them for tithes, precisely on the same principle that it had previously laid hold of all other known produce—not because a tenth of them had been assigned to pious uses by some private proprietor five or six hundred years before, but because public authority had ordained that every man in the realm should devote the tenth of his annual increase to religious and charitable ends.[1]

4. Passing on, now, from the cultivated to the uncultivated portion of the proprietor's estate we

---

[1] The Courts of Equity recognised the late introduction of turnips and potatoes, upon general historical evidence, without requiring proof of the time when they were first cultivated.

stumble on another class of titheable article in the shape of *furze* and *broom*. Wherever these were cut and sold, they paid tithe—but when burnt in a house of husbandry, or used for sheep pens, or for burning lime for manure, within the same parish in which they were cut, they were exempt. These, we fancy, tell their own tale distinctly enough, and the reader will agree with us that it is in unison with all that has gone before.

5. Of *hemp* and *flax*, which were not titheable in kind, but at a fixed sum per acre[1]—(still more modern additions, we may add, to English farm produce than turnips and potatoes)—*madder*[2] (to which the same remark applies), *wood*, *teazles* (quite recent), and *saffron*, we will not weary the reader with details—for we should only be retreading oft-trodden ground.

6. *Honey* and *wax* come into the category of things titheable—but not bees. Our pious ancestors we suppose, deemed sweets and candles more likely to comfort and sustain the Church than stings. The law books inform us that this class of produce is titheable by *common right*.[3]

7. And now for *hops*. They were no doubt known in this country tolerably early, for they are indi-

---

[1] The first statute on the tithing of these articles was, 3 Will. and Mary, cap. 3, made for seven years, fixing the rate of payment at four shillings an acre. By the 11 and 12 Will. III. cap. 16, made perpetual by 1 Geo. I. stat. 2, cap. 26, s. 2, the sum of five shillings per acre of hemp and flax is directed to be paid by the cultivator as tithe to the parson.

[2] A temporary provision in favour of the cultivation of madder, was made by 5 Geo. III. c. 18. which was not renewed on expiry.

[3] Honey was titheable by measure and wax by weight. But no tenth was payable for the tenth swarm of bees, because they are *feræ naturæ*.

genous, but before Henry the VIII.'s time, only as "a venomous weed." They probably never came under cultivation till about Elizabeth's reign, and then, perhaps, in response to the fostering care of the statute 5 and 6 Edward VI. cap. 5—at any rate, not till long after the settlement of the tithe system.[1] They were nevertheless made titheable as soon as they became an article of profit—not by private bounty, but by the generative force of the principles of *public law*.

8. *Seeds*, such as rape seed, turnip seed, and clover seed, and *acorns* and *mast* of trees[2] (when they were gathered and sold) conclude our long list of articles swept *by law* within the meshes of small prædial tithes. Ancient or modern, rare or plentiful, profitable to man or beast—it was all the same. If they grew, and were made gain of, the Church claimed her share, and the law allowed it.

MIXED TITHES.

These tithes were so called because they were held to arise upon things partly prædial and partly personal—prædial in respect of the ground on which the animals furnishing them were depastured—and personal, in respect of the constant care which such animals require. They were, however, to be paid

---

[1] The Courts, both of Law and Equity, take judicial notice that hops were not introduced into this country until after the time of legal memory, and, consequently, cannot be the subject of any immemorial custom.

[2] But when acorns or mast of trees fell and were eaten by hogs, no tithes were paid.

without any deduction on account of the labour and expense they might involve. The class comprised the following items, which we shall dispatch as cursorily as possible.

1. *Milk*—about the right mode of paying which the law continued down to comparatively recent times very uncertain. At length it was settled that the whole of the morning's and evening's milking of every tenth day was to be set out for the tithe-owner, which, unless special custom ruled otherwise, the parson was bound to remove from the farm in his own pails before the usual hour for the next milking came round—and where the cows were fed in one parish and milked in another the tithes were deemed payable to the parson of the parish in which they were milked.[1] Ewe's milk even was said to be due of common right, and has been, in some instances, both claimed and allowed. But cheese, butter, and cream, were not titheable in kind, the common law, having made the milk of which they were manufactured payable in kind throughout the year.

2. The next article of this class, *wool*, was subject to tithe immediately after it had been clipped, and was held due to the parson of the parish in which the sheep were shorn. The farmer, however, if he chose, in a *bonâ fide* course of shepherding, to shear his sheep round their necks, in order to preserve them and their fleece from brambles was not required

---

[1] Tithes were payable of milk, notwithstanding the cows might have been fed on after-pasture, or on hay, or turnips drawn from the ground, which had before paid tithe, for the milk was regarded as of a distinct nature, and the tithe was payable for the produce of the animal itself, and not for the grass or herbage eaten.

to pay tithe of the clippings! The Church asserted her claim even to this vexatious extent, but the law did not allow it.[1] Historical evidence exists of the high value of wool in ancient times.[2]

3. *The young of animals* are included in this class—namely, lambs, pigs, calves, colts, and kids.[3] Law has determined in the case of lambs, that the right of tithe accrued to the tithe-owner at the animal's birth, but that he was neither bound nor allowed to demand his right until the lamb had reached a proper age for weaning. As to the selection of the tenth (where there were ten) custom decided the rule for each locality. Pigs, calves, colts and kids were dealt with in an analogous manner. One rule however, set forth in 2 and 3 Edward. VI. cap. 13, s. 4, was equally applicable to the young of all domesticated browsing animals — namely, that when they pastured on waste or common ground, the parish of which was not certainly known, tithe of their

---

[1] In the case of Dent *v.* Salvin, it was ruled that if a parishioner cut the dirty locks from his sheep for their better preservation from vermin, without fraud, no tithes should be paid of them. Think of taking such a question into court!

[2] Edward III. sent the Bishop of Lincoln and the Earls of Northampton and Suffolk, with 10,000 sacks of wool into Brabant, to make retainers in High Germany, which they sold for 40*l.* a sack, computed to have been about 2*s.* 2¼*d.*, of the then currency, per pound.

[3] By the constitutions of Gray, Archbishop of York, in A.D. 1250, and of Winchelsea, Archbishop of Canterbury, in 1305, it was ordained that if there were six lambs or other, a halfpenny for each lamb should be paid to the parson; if seven or more, that the seventh lamb should be paid, the parson giving back to the parishioner three halfpence when there are seven lambs, a penny when there were eight, and a halfpenny when there were nine. The clergy of our pious forefathers looked well after their temporal rights, and claimed to be thereby doing God service! The young of other domesticated animals were analogously dealt with.

increase was due to the "parson, vicar, proprietor, portionary owner, or other their farmers or deputies, of the parish, hamlet, town, or other place, where the owner of the said cattle inhabits or dwells." It will hardly be contended that the lords of manors in olden times gave the Church a right to tithes accruing on commons beyond the limits of their own estates. The origin of tithes in public law offers the only rational explanation of this, and numberless other provisions, affecting this class of tithe property.

4. We finish up this course of mixed tithes with *eggs* and *pigeons*. Tithes were held to be due of common right of the eggs of all tame and domestic fowls — but not of pheasants or partridges, although kept in inclosures — nor of tame ducks kept for the service of a decoy. Where tithes were paid of eggs, however, none were paid of their young. Turkeys, although introduced into this country since legal memory, were made titheable, as were pigeons if kept in a dovecote whenever they were not eaten in the family, but sold.

PERSONAL TITHES.

1. By a constitution of Archbishop Winchelsea, it is ordained that "personal tithes shall be paid of artificers and merchandisers, that is, of the *gain of their commerce;* as also of carpenters, smiths, masons, weavers, innkeepers and all other workmen and hirelings, that they pay tithes of their *wages*, unless such hireling shall give something in certain to the use, or for the light of the church, if the rector shall so think

proper." How far this ecclesiastical law was ever enforced must remain matter of conjecture, though it points clearly enough to the origin of the tithe system. Its force, however, was limited by the statute 2 and 3 Edward VI. cap. 13, s. 7, to such " as heretofore within these forty years have accustomably used to pay such personal tithes, or, of right, ought to pay (other than such as be common day labourers)."[1] Hunting, hawking, angling and fowling fell under the rules of personal tithes.

2. Unless a clear custom to the contrary could be established, the tithe of *fish* taken in the sea was payable to the parson of the parish where the fishermen resided.

3. *Mills*, likewise, paid tithes — or in other words, the miller was liable to the tithe-owner for a tenth of his nett gains.[2] But from early times the right of the Church to this due was vigorously and constantly disputed, until the statute of *articuli cleri* was passed in the reign of Edward II., A.D. 1315. The effect of that Act was to exempt all mills of all kinds which had not customarily paid tithes before the passing of

---

[1] " And where handicraftmen have used to pay their tithes within this forty years, the same custom of tithes is to be observed; and if any person refuse to pay his personal tithes, &c., it shall be lawful for the Ordinary of the same diocess to call the same party before him, and by his discretion to examine him by all lawful and reasonable means, other than by the party's own corporal oath, concerning the true payment of the said tithes." 2 & 3 Edw. VI. cap. 13.

[2] Here was another contest carried on through a long course of years between the clergy and the laity, settled at length by a sort of compromise. The history, as traced in church canons, and the decisions of law courts, and parliamentary proceedings is remarkably suggestive; but one thing it does not suggest, namely, that tithe endowments sprung out of the individual liberality of lords of manors.

it, and to fasten the obligation on all corn mills erected subsequently to that date. Even any improvement of machinery in the mill — such as the addition of another pair of stones — has been claimed by the tithe-owner as liable for tithe, although not certainly allowed.

OBSERVATIONS ON THE ABOVE.

Those of our readers who have been at the pains of following us through this long catalogue of titheable things, can be at no loss in coming to a decided conclusion on the question as to whether tithes were originally bestowed on parish churches by private endowment. The vast range over which the claim extended, and the multiplicity of personal interests which it affected, are of themselves sufficient to prove that it could never have had its commencement in the grants of individual piety or superstition. Else, how is it that the list was almost uniformly identical in every parish in the kingdom? In the conveyances of tithes arbitrarily made to religious houses by individuals, nothing is more common than a specification of things on which tithes were granted.[1] How did it happen that tithes annexed to parish churches, both great and small, were almost invariably taken on precisely the same list? And what is still more suggestive, how came it to pass that, on any legal dispute as to liability of payment, neither ecclesiastical nor civil court ever inquired what might have been the intentions of the supposed

---

[1] See note 2. p. 77.

founder of the endowment, but always guided its decision by common law principles and precedents? We have law cases on the subject of tithes running back to within a short distance of the Norman Conquest, but not one of them throws out so much as a hint that our law courts dealt with them on the supposition that this kind of property originated in the will of individuals. We doubt whether friend or foe had ever broached such a theory before the learned but speculative and paradoxical Selden first sported it in the earlier part of the seventeenth century.

But with regard to a number of the titheable things above enumerated, it is certain that individual benevolence not only did not, but *could not* have devoted the tenth "to God and the Church." We have specified several of those articles, such as turnips, potatoes, hops, hemp, flax, and several garden fruits and vegetables, which were either wholly unknown in England, or, if known, were not turned into sources of gain till long after the establishment of the tithe system. But we have made but a passing remark on *personal* tithes. Will any man in his senses pretend that pious lords of manors, of their own private will, gave to the clergy the right, for all future time, to mulct the artificers resident in their parishes of a tenth of their wages? or assigned to the Church a tenth of the fish caught in the sea? or subjected millers to the ecclesiastical impost from A.D. 1315? or "gave a tenth of the spoils" of all hawking, hunting, fishing, and fowling? It matters nothing to the argument that in some of these cases tithe was seldom paid, and the claim for it soon ceased. The claim was *made* by ecclesiastical law. On what ground? On the pretext that the right had been granted by some lord of the manor? Never—but on the ground of ecclesiastical right having its roots in the divine law. We take this part of the argument, therefore, to be demonstrative. Added to what has preceded it, it leaves not so much as an inch of standing ground to the advocates of the private origin of tithe endowments. But if a shred of probability yet remains to uphold that figment of modern ecclesiastical conjecture, we undertake to demolish it entirely, and we hope at much less length, in the next chapter.

CHAP. VI.

MODERN EXPANSION AND EXTENSION OF TITHE ENDOWMENTS.

WE have spent enough time over this theory, so coolly assumed, so artfully insinuated, so boldly iterated, of late, in behalf of the Established Church — that its parochial endowments originated in private lay liberality. We have already done more than is necessary to disprove it. But we know our men — and therefore we propose to submit to their consideration the following facts.

The tithes now in the Church of England's enjoyment are a certain proportion derived from the annual produce of the soil under cultivation in this country. In England and Wales (for we confine our attention to them) it is estimated by the highest authorities that there are from twelve to thirteen millions of acres under the plough, and from ten to eleven laid down in grass — in all, speaking in round numbers, about twenty-four millions of acres under cultivation. We have advisedly adopted the lowest estimate. In the evidence laid before the Committee of the House of Lords on Waste Lands, as far back as the year 1827, a gentleman who was a surveyor by profession, and who had travelled 15,000 miles in order to get his *data*, placed an estimate before their lordships, which brought up the cultivated land in England and Wales to 28,749,000 acres.[1] This, we have little doubt, was a somewhat extravagant estimate. Mr. Caird sets down the extent of land under the plough in 1850–51 at 13,817,000 acres[2], and Mr. M'Culloch at 12,700,000 acres.[3] The "Times" of January 4, 1860, in an article on the steam-plough, puts down the whole arable land in Great Britain at 19,000,000 acres, and the grass land at little less.[4] On the whole, then, we are exceedingly moderate in estimating the land, both arable and pasture, under cultivation in England and Wales, at the present moment, and paying tithe or rent-charge on its annual produce, at 24,000,000 acres.[5]

Now, from the year 1760 to 1849 there were passed by the Imperial Parliament no fewer than 3867 Enclosure Bills, bringing under cultivation

---

[1] Report of Lord's Committee on Waste Lands, 1827. Mr. Cowling's estimate is as follows.

CULTIVATED LAND.

	Acres.
England	25,632,000
Wales	3,117,000
Total	28,749,000

[2] Caird's "Agriculture," p. 522. The estimate is for A.D. 1850–1, for England only.

[3] M'Culloch's "Commercial Dictionary" for 1859. The estimate is for the year 1858, and refers to England only.

[4] Deducting Scotland and Ireland, the estimate for England would closely approach the two former.

[5] The proportion of grass land to arable is commonly taken as about five to six.

7,350,577 acres.[1] If, therefore, we set down the number of acres redeemed from waste during the last hundred years at eight millions of acres, we shall probably be within the mark. But eight is just one-third of twenty-four. This disposes at one fell swoop of a third of the tithe property of the kingdom, *as having been brought into existence within the last century.* Shall we be told that this third had its origin in private lay liberality? Where are the legal documents? It is not far to go back for them—let them be produced! We are utterly ashamed to dwell upon so plain a case.

Let us take another step! The Act 2 and 3 Edward VI. cap. 13, s. 5, has this provision:—" All such barren or waste ground (other than such as be discharged from the payment of tithes by Act of Parliament) which before this time have lain barren and paid no tithes by reason of the same barrenness and now be or hereafter shall be, improved and converted into arable or meadow, shall, after the end and term of seven years next after such improvement fully ended and determined, pay tithe for the corn and hay growing upon the same." [2] We pre-

---

[1] The first Enclosure Bill was passed in the year 1710, in the eighth year of Queen Anne's reign. Most of the modern enclosures, however, have been made under the authority of the General Enclosure Act of 41 Geo. III. cap. 109.

[2] The common law, unquestionably, made all such land titheable, immediately upon being brought under cultivation. The statute law merely exempts for the first seven years. But, as it is universally agreed that it was intended principally for the advancement of agriculture, the conclusion to which we have come as to the comparatively modern origin of the greater proportion of tithe property, and as to the impossibility of its having originated in individual grants of land proprietors, is perfectly legitimate.

sume that tithe of the annual produce of lands brought under cultivation since this enactment may be fairly traced back for its origin to this statute. What proportion of land was under cultivation when this Act was passed? The population in A.D. 1575 was 5,274,000 souls [1]— and in the beginning of Edward VI.'s reign could not have appreciably exceeded 5,000,000. As England was not at that time a corn-exporting country, and the people can hardly be supposed to have required, or to have eaten and drunk, a greater quantity of bread and meat and beer, in proportion, than now, it is a high estimate which computes the extent of land then under the plough, or depastured, at 6,000,000 acres. In other words, eighteen of the twenty-four millions of acres now under cultivation, or *just three-fourths*, have been redeemed from waste since the passing of the Act of Parliament referred to above. There remains, therefore, only one-fourth of the tithe property now existing which could by any possibility have grown out of lay liberality. The other three-fourths are directly traceable, not to private grants — not even to custom or common law — but to the legislation of Parliament. Three-fourths of the parochial endowments of the Church of England have their root in an Act of Parliament passed a little more than three hundred years ago. Let that

---

[1] Chalmers' "Domestic Economy of Great Britain and Ireland," pp. 4, 14, 38. This is a very high estimate, for in the "Observations on the Register Abstracts," 1801, the population of England in A.D. 1700 is set down at only 5,475,000. Froude in his "History of England" computes the population of this country at the commencement of Henry VIII.'s reign, as somewhat under 5,000,000.

CHAP. VI.   AREA OF TITHEABLE PROPERTY.   59

fact be explained away, if it can be, by those who contend for the sacredness and inalienability of tithe endowments, on the ground of their having been consecrated by individual piety.

From the Reformation back to the time of King John, when lords of manors, as we shall see in the next chapter, ceased to appropriate their tithes arbitrarily, will take us back somewhat more than another three hundred years. But, according to a calculation founded on a Subsidy Roll of A.D. 1377, still extant, the population in that year was 2,353,000 souls — and about A.D. 1200 would be about 2,000,000.[1] Considering that during that period famines were frequent, it is difficult to imagine that the extent of land then under cultivation could have reached 2,500,000 acres. Now, all the increase of tithe property accruing to the Church from A.D. 1200, when there may have been about 2,500,000 acres cultivated, down to Edward VI.'s reign, when there were, as we have shown, about 6,000,000 acres, came out of *law*, not out of private benevolence — for individual and arbitrary disposal of tithes was not known during that interval of time.[2] Full eight-ninths, then, of tithe property are directly traceable up to their source in *public law* — that is, 21,500,000 acres out of 24,000,000, on the produce of which rent-charges are now held due to the Church, have been redeemed

---

[1] Cove's "Essays on the Revenues of the Church of England," third edition, 1816, p. 240; see note 7.

[2] From the Council of Lateran A.D. 1215, there is no historical evidence whatever of any arbitrary disposal of tithes by individual grants.

from waste, and hence become titheable, *since* the age in which private gifts of tithes, by deed or grant, were customarily made, or were lawful. And we shall presently point out how little reason there is to believe that the parochial tithe due on the the remaining 2,500,000 acres originated in any other source. The private origin of parochial tithe endowments has only a shadow of argument in its favour, in respect to about a tenth of the whole — the other nine-tenths are put out of court by the evidence of facts.

What will be the next pretence of the upholders of the private theory? We can guess. They will say that the lay owners of landed estates gave to the Church not only tithe of the then cultivated portion of them, but a title to take tithes whenever the uncultivated and waste portions of their respective lordships should be redeemed by agriculture — in a word, that their generosity and piety freely disposed of, not merely then existing actualities, but future possibilities through all succeeding generations. Now we will not stay to contest the right of lords of manors to determine what conditions should attach to waste lands when brought, ages after their day, into cultivation. But it is worthy of observation that by common law, and from time immemorial, the tithes of forest lands, and of lands not included within a parish, belonged to the Crown — or rather the title to tithes did.[1] The Crown, as

---

[1] See Burn's "Ecclesiastical Law," art. "Tithes," iii. p. 683, and all the other law books.

representative of the State, that is of the people in their civil capacity, held the fee-simple of the tithes which might at any time be derived from lands not as yet parcelled out by parochial boundaries. Now by far the larger proportion of our parishes have come into existence *qua* parishes since the period at which the tithe system was adopted. For it was subsequently to A.D. 1200 that most of our parish churches, having the right of baptistry and burial ground, were founded — and the territory of the demesnes and tenancies of the lords of the manor who erected such churches, constituted the parochial limits.[1] We shall not be far from the mark then, in saying that the fee-simple of the largest proportion of tithes *in posse* which have since, by cultivation of the land, become tithes *in esse*, was originally held by the Crown in trust for the nation. As an illustration, we may refer to the Act 15 Car. II. cap. 17, " for settling of the drainage of the great level of the fens, called Bedford Level," in which it is enacted that " no ascertaining or dividing the said drained or new improved lands" by the Commissioners appointed by the Act " shall conclude the King's Majesty, his heirs, &c." . . . . " as to the bounds of parishes " . . . . so far, at least, as they may affect the king's " right to tithes." Indeed, *waste* land was always, in the eye of law, synonymous with land unenclosed, and unbounded by hedge or ditch, which no man could tell to whom it cer-

---

[1] Selden's " History of Tithes," chap. xi. s. 4.
[2] Eagle's " Law of Tithes," chap. iii. s. 5.

tainly belonged.¹ Generally speaking it was extra-parochial — and, as we have seen, the title to its tithes *in posse* resided in the Crown.

We resist the strong temptation pressing upon us to add to the bare logic of the foregoing paragraphs anything merely pictorial and illustrative, or we might fill many pages with sketches of the physical condition of England in bygone times, which would help the reader to realise the exceedingly gradual, and unsuspectedly recent, process by which the Church of England has come into possession of her present parochial endowments. We might take him back but a short two hundred years, and point out to him a region of twenty-five miles circumference, within sight of this metropolis, within which there were, even at that comparatively modern date, but three houses and scarcely any enclosed fields. We might travel with him along roads which at this day pass through well-cultivated lands, upon which he would not two centuries back have been able to see, on either side of the way, more than an occasional inclosure for forty miles together. We might prove to him the vast difference between the extent of agriculture in those days and in these, from the number

---

¹ The legal definitions of barren, waste, and heath land laid down by the Courts about thirty years after the passing of the Act 2 & 3 Edw. VI. cap. 13, s. 5, is as follows:—"*Barren* ground is understood by the opinion and judgment of the common law, to be whereof no profit arises or grows; and that ground which is stubbed, and after bears either corn or grain, is not barren. *Waste*, is understood such ground as no man challenges as his own, or no man can tell to whom it certainly belongs, and lies uninclosed and unbounded by hedge or ditch; but the ground that lies inclosed and hedged and ditched in, and the lord known, is no waste ground. *Heath* ground is understood that ground that is dispersed, and lies at common."

of wild animals to be met with in forest and fen, on moor and heath, in swamp and warren—wild boars, wolves, foxes, red deer, fen eagles, bustards, and cranes.[1] But were we to go back to the earlier days in which the tithe laws originated, we should show him a picture of Nature in her undress such as he would not readily forget. North of the Trent especially, he would find almost the whole district wild and barbarous—so little redeemed from waste, as to furnish secure retreats for marauders even from the powerful instincts of bloodhounds—the seats of the gentry strongly fortified, and the farmhouses clustering about them for protection—and judges on circuit carrying their provisions with them, and escorted from town to town through the desolate country, by sheriffs commanding a considerable armed force.[2]

And yet, it is in these times, and amid such surrounding circumstances, that modern Churchmen pretend to have discovered the beginning of parochial endowments in the pious liberality of individual land-proprietors. Not a parish in the kingdom is without its Church endowment—not a parish without an endowment of precisely the same character—a tenth of the annual produce, neither more nor less. No matter at what date the parish came into being as such—it always had a land-owner who voluntarily devoted his tenth to the Church. North, south, east, or west, it mattered not—in the ninth century, or in the fourteenth, or in any intervening

---

[1] See Macaulay's "History of England," vol. i. chap. iii. from whose vivid description most of the above particulars are gleaned.
[2] Ibid.

period, it mattered not—whensoever and wheresoever out of waste and barrenness there came cultivation and profit, then and there, without so much as a single exception, there was invariably a "pious ancestor," who gave of his own to ecclesiastical uses that which every other land-owner gave. Not one missed—not one cultivated estate was exempt, save by a subsequent process of redemption. *Credat Judæus!* The theory was invented to serve a purpose, but it certainly does not serve the purpose of explaining or illustrating history. A more utterly ridiculous figment of fancy was never sported—nor one which, when fairly grappled with, more hopelessly collapsed.

CHAP. VII.

ARBITRARY ASSIGNMENT OF TITHES.

SUFFICIENT evidence, we think, has been produced in support of our position that the tithe system of this country has its true foundations in public law; nevertheless, the opposite opinion, that it may be ultimately traced back to private liberality, widely obtains. There must be some reason for this, some facts which may account for it; these, accordingly, we proceed to examine.

During the whole period of English history intervening between the Heptarchy and Magna Charta, there was, as we have seen, an unequal and various struggle between public authority, whether in Church or State, and private right, in regard to the payment of tithes. This antagonism must ever be borne in mind by those who would rightly interpret the ecclesiastical facts of the period. In the first attempts to establish a universal obligation to pay her demands, the Church, although supported by the authority of the State, achieved but a partial and imperfect success.[1] As the spiritual power of the Popedom steadily increased, however, the rights which the laity had asserted for themselves were one

[1] See Chap. IV. *passim.*

after another extinguished. There were fluctuations as usual, in this ceaseless contest—authority being sometimes, and in regard to some things, paramount, whilst occasionally, and in regard to other matters, resistance was, for a time at least, successfully maintained.[1] But, in the long run, ecclesiastical power established a decided ascendancy over lay recusancy — and private rights succumbed beneath the double pressure of Church censures and the penalties of civil law.

The results of this struggle (still keeping within the historical period already marked out) were twofold. On the one hand, the obligation of subjects to surrender a tenth of their annual increase or profits to pious uses, was everywhere established, and came to be generally recognised—but, on the other, the right of the landowner to pay his tithes, and the tithes of his tenants and villains[2], to any church or

---

[1] Instances in which Church authority either speedily or eventually proved too strong for the successful resistance of the laity, will be found in such cases as the following. When laymen first began to build parish oratories or churches in their lordships, some of them claimed an interest in the oblations received from Christian devotion in their churches, similar to that which had been previously enjoyed by the bishop of the diocese. This was especially the case on the continent, but was soon put down by Church constitutions. But the right claimed by the laity to collate to a living so as to give the incumbent full title to the endowments without the aid of the bishop or other ecclesiastic, was stoutly maintained for a considerable period. In fact, in older times, the incumbent, as usufructuary, held immediately from the patron as proprietor. This practice, however, was ultimately overruled by pontifical decrees and church canons. Selden, chap. vi. sect. 3. The laity, as will have been seen in a foregoing chapter, were more successful in regard to the tithing of timber, ancient mills, &c.

[2] The lords of manors disposed of the tithes of their tenants and villains without the smallest ceremony. Take, as a single example among several, the following extract from the Leominster Chartulary. Walter Clifford

religious house which he thought fit to select, was successfully asserted down to about A.D. 1200. Between payment and *non*-payment of a tenth for religious purposes no choice was left him—no *right* of choice was ultimately made good. On this question the doctrine, the constitutions, the canons, and the censures of the Church, backed, moreover, as we have seen, by the power of the magistrate, effectually silenced the objections and protests of individual right—not all at once, it is true—not equally in every part of the realm—but, in the course of a century or two, so generally, as to make *the principle* of paying a tenth for pious uses a law of conscience, and a part of the common law of the land.[1] Thus far, the ecclesiastical power was triumphant.

But the laity, in recognising the theory of religious obligation, chose to discharge that obligation in favour of such pious uses as they themselves preferred—and, spite of canonical prohibitions, preserved that freedom, more or less, down to King John's time. Of this fact the evidence is abundant. Thus Pope Innocent III., in one of his Decretal Epistles to the Archbishop of Canterbury, writes:— "Many persons in your diocess distribute their tithes according to their own choice."[2] Wickliffe also, in his complaint to the king and parliament, under Richard II., distinctly refers to the ancient practice:

gives "Ecclesiæ de Leominstre, decimam de tota Hamenesca, tam de dominio *quam de villanis suis*, de omnibus unde Decimæ dantur." Selden, chap. ii. sect. 1, *passim*.

[1] Prideaux's "Original and Right of Tithes," chap. v. from p. 191 to p. 199.

[2] Innocent III. in epist. decret. lib. ii. p. 452, edit. Colon.

"Ah, Lord Jesu Christ," he exclaims, "sith within few years, men payed their tithes and offerings at their own will free to good men, and able to great worship of God, to profit and fairness of Holy Church, fighting in earth."[1] So, in the Year Book, 7 Edward III., Parning, then Lord Chancellor, is reported as saying, "In olden time, before a constitution recently made by the Pope, the patron of a church could grant tithes within his parish to another parish."[2] Herle confirms this *dictum*, observing that "it is against reason that a man cannot give his alms to whomsoever he will."[3] Ludlow, Judge of Assize, in the same reign, tells us emphatically that "in former times every man could grant the tithes of his land to what church he would"[4]—"which is true," remarks Judge Brooke, in his abridged report of the case. Dyer's authority is equally explicit.[5]

"However," says Selden, in summing up the historical evidence on this point, "it is most clear (let froward ignorance, as it can, continue to oppose the assertion) that for two hundred years at least before the time of the Council of Lateran, held under the same pope (Innocent III. A.D. 1215) "arbitrary

---

[1] Apud Selden, chap. x. sect. 2.

[2] "En auncien temps, devant un constitution de novelle fait per le Pape, un patron d'un Eglise puit granter Dismes, dans mesme le paroche à un altre paroche." Edw. III. fol. 5.

[3] 7 Edw. III. fol. 5 a. He says, "Que home ne purra my granter ses almoignes a que il vouldra."

[4] 44 Edw. III. 5, 22. His words are "En auncien temps chescun home purroit graunter les Dismes de sa terre à quel Eglise il voudroit."

[5] 7 Edw. VI. Dyer, fol. 84 b. He says that before the Council of Lateran, lay owners might dispose of their tithes, "cuicunque ecclesiæ secundum meliorem devotionem."

consecrations of tithes with us were frequent, and practised, as well of *positive right* (if we may take that for right in things subject to human disposition, which general consent of the State allowed—as no man that knows what makes a positive right can deny) as of *fact*."[1]

We propose now to trace the visible effects produced by the modifying influence of this arbitrariness on the part of the laity in the disposal of their tithe, upon their practice as brought about by canonical and legal obligation. In order to this, we must first of all realise to ourselves the ordinary circumstances under which, in individual instances, tithes, during this period, came into being. Here, for example, is a lord of an estate, comprising, it may be, some thousands of acres, partly uncleared, partly cultivated. He has his tenants and his villains, or serfs, and he exercises over them a tolerably despotic dominion. That estate constitutes what is now called a parish, and the limits of the one determine the boundaries of the other.[2] Let us suppose the lord to be a devout Churchman. In proportion as he gets his estate under cultivation, his family, his household retainers, his tenants, and his serfs become more numerous. The collegiate church of the district is far away, and it is but occasionally that one of the clergy from the cathedral can visit the estate to minister the Word and the sacraments to the rural

---

[1] Selden, chap. x. sect. 2, at the end.

[2] Selden, chap. ix. sect. 4. The facts in this paragraph are chiefly gleaned from Selden. Some of them are concisely stated in the article "Parish," in Burn's "Ecclesiastical Law."

colony.[1] With the assent of the bishop[2], the lord of the estate builds a church; and then, instead of contributing his tithes and offerings to the common fund of the bishopric, he retains them, in fee, for his own church.[3] The bishop is induced to consecrate the building, and if it have a baptistry and burial-ground attached to it, it becomes, to all intents and purposes, a parish church.[4] The advowson (that is the right of nominating the parson who shall have the usufruct of the tithes and offerings, or such portions of them as the landlord may determine, and in return for which the parson is to render his religious service) he claims as his own—but it is necessary for the bishop to ordain the priest to that church, and in all spiritual affairs the incumbent

---

[1] " In these primitive times of the English-Saxon Church, the Bishop and the whole clergy of the diocese were as one body, living upon their endowments (bestowed on the bishopric), and their treasure that came from the sundry places of devotion whither some one or other of them at the Bishop's appointment, was sent to preach the word and minister the sacraments, every clerk having his dividend for his maintenance." Selden, chap. ix. sect. 2. He quotes Bede as his authority.

[2] " No layman could of himself make any building to be a church without the Bishop's consecration of it." Selden, chap. vi. sect. 3, p. 85.

[3] " Every man, questionless, would have been the unwillinger to have specially endowed the church, founded for the holy use, chiefly of him, his family, and tenants, if withal he might not have had the liberty to have given his incumbent there resident, a special and several maintenance, which could not have been had the former community of the of the clergies' revenue still remained." This passage implies that the tithes now settled by the lord of the manor on the incumbent had been previously paid to the common fund of the bishopric. It is extracted from Selden, chap. ix. sect. 4, p. 260.

[4] " Right of sepulture was and regularly is a character of a parish church or *Ecclesiæ*, as it is commonly distinguished from *capella*; and anciently if a *quare impedit* had been brought for a church, whereas the defendant pretended it to be a chapel only, the issue was not so much whether it were a church or chapel, as whether it had *Baptisterium* or *Sepulturum*, or no." Selden, ibid. p. 265.

(nominated by the proprietor, and receiving from him his sole title to the temporalities) is responsible to the bishop.[1] Every acre of the estate that comes newly into cultivation, serves to swell the tithe revenue, and is due by canonical and civil law to pious uses—but it rests with the proprietor whether the whole tithe accruing from his estate, old and new, shall be settled on the parson of the parish, or whether some portion of it shall not be consecrated to special objects.[2]

In those days, however, as now, landed estates did not always fall into the hands of godly proprietors. But tithes were claimed, and, as far as law could reach, received, of sinners as well as saints, whether the lord's estate was only visited from the cathedral church as opportunity might allow, or whether a resident clergyman and a parish church existed. In the former case, the whole ecclesiastical income of the parish went to the bishop; who, in case he had himself been provided for by a landed estate (as he commonly had been long before A.D. 1200), apportioned the fund of his diocese between the clergy who lived with him and who carried the ordinances of religion to destitute districts, the building, repairing, and decoration of churches in the diocese, and the relief of the poor. Now, a land proprietor who

---

[1] The custom of the times is indicated by the language used in a deed wherein Thomas, Archbishop of York, confirms to the priory of Durham all churches then, or thereafter to be, appropriated to them. Respecting the vicars whom the monks might place in these churches, the deed says, "qui mihi et successoribus meis de cura tantum intendant animarum, ipsis vero de omnibus cæteris Eleemosynis et Beneficiis." Hoveden's "Annals," part 1, fol. 263.

[2] See below, note.

erected a church on his estate, claimed, and for a considerable period, maintained, the same power of apportioning the tithe of his parish as the bishop had been wont to exercise in respect of the common fund of his diocese. . One-third of the tithe he usually allotted to the parson he had installed in the benefice, reserving the two-thirds, not ostensibly to his own use, but to the reparation of the edifice, and to the assistance of the indigent.[1] If he sometimes forgot to discharge these burdens adequately or at all, he quieted his conscience with the reflection that he was only repaying himself for his outlay in rearing the ecclesiastical edifice. It is certain that on the continent, and it is more than probable that in England, during the earlier part of this interval of time, "the erecting of churches," as Selden says, "became amongst some, to be rather gainful than devout—for the patron would arbitrarily divide to the incumbent, and take the rest to his own use."[2] Two or three canons of the Roman Church refer pointedly, and in express terms, to this practice, and condemn it.[3]

That the practice was not unknown here may be clearly enough gathered from Lindwood, who says, "For before that Council" (of Lateran) "laymen could *retain their tithes in fee,* and give them to

---

[1] "But this tripartite division soon occasioned great disorders; for the lay patrons did from hence infer, that a third part of the revenues of a church was sufficient for the supply of it, and they undertook to dispose of the two remaining parts; at first pretending to apply them to the like pious uses; but then by degrees detaining them in their own hands." Burn's "Ecclesiastical Law," art. "Appropriations."

[2] Selden, chap. vi. sect. 3.

[3] The second Council of Bracara and the ninth Council of Toledo.

another church or monastery."[1] And this brings us to the common practice during the whole period of which we are treating, of *special and arbitrary consecrations of tithes* to religious houses — a practice, we suspect, which has given rise to the notion that the endowment of parish churches had its origin in the voluntary liberality of lay patrons — whereas, carefully looked at, it proves the very reverse. We shall, therefore, set forth, in the first place, the facts of the case, and shall afterwards note some of the conclusions to which they lead us.[2]

During the period to which we still confine our attention, monasteries, convents, abbacies, and various other kinds of religious houses, sprung up in England in great numbers. The heads and members of these houses, affecting greater sanctity than the parish clergy, and bound by the rules of their order to a stricter religious life, obtained greater influence over the lay mind of that superstitious age. As one means of increasing their own power and wealth, they incited their benefactors to assign to them, either in whole or in part, the tithes accruing on their several estates, the advowsons of churches, and, after the Norman Conquest, churches and their tithes absolutely to their own use. The monastery or collegiate body to which such assignments were made,

---

[1] "Ante illud Concilium bene potuerunt Laici Decimas in feudum retinere, et eas alteri Ecclesiæ vel Monasterio dare." Apud Selden, chap. x. sect. 2, p. 293.

[2] The whole subject is largely discussed by Selden — and, indeed, it seems probable that it was with a view to establish his theory, founded upon this exceptional practice, that he wrote his celebrated book on Tithes.

usually appointed clergy to perform religious service in the parishes in which they had the advowson, or where the church and tithes belonged to them *in pleno jure,* either remunerating such clergy by a wretched stipend, or assigning to them the small tithes, and what were called the altarages — that is, offerings of a minor kind brought to the altar. Such clergy were called vicars — and when a settled maintenance out of the tithe of the parish was alloted to them, their benefices were styled "perpetual vicarages." These men performed the spiritual duty in their parishes in lieu of the monks who swept into their treasury the greater portion of the ecclesiastical income.[1]

It seems to have been quite a passion with the laity of those times to assign the churches they had erected, and the tithes of their estates, to these religious houses — insomuch that, in an age or two, the monastic orders had absorbed well nigh a half of the advowsons in the kingdom, and had *appropriated* or, in other words, held as their absolute property and to their own use, above a third, and those the richest, of the benefices in England.[2]

But these monks grounded their right to parochial

---

[1] The statements contained in this paragraph are derived from Selden; Burn's "Ecclesiastical Law," article on "Appropriation;" Prideaux's "Original and Right of Tithes," and Sir Simon Degge's "Parson's Counsellor."

[2] "And by these means in an age or two above one half of the parochial churches in England came to be lodged in the power of cathedrals and monasteries." ... "And so this practice, which crept in with William the Conqueror, in a few reigns became the custom of the land, and the infection spread, until within the space of 300 years, above a third part, and those generally the richest benefices of England, became appropriated." Burn's "Eccles. Law," art. "Appropriation," i. pp. 70, 72.

tithes upon a different right of tenure to that relied upon by the parochial clergy. The latter, after about forty years' prescription, held whatever they enjoyed, not by special deed of gift, but by *common law*.[1] A monastery, if challenged at law respecting the right by which it claimed certain tithes, was compelled to produce the deeds in which the conveyance had been made to it — a parochial parson, on the contrary, was always presumed to be entitled to the tithes of his parish, and could only be ousted by the production of the legal instrument by which a special grant of them had been made to some other ecclesiastical party.[2] Hence, these religious houses very carefully preserved such documents, as evidence of their title, and copies of many of them, as also some originals, have been handed down to our times.

These chartularies, as they were called, contain extremely curious and interesting illustrations of the caprice of our pious ancestors in distributing the tithes which the law compelled them to pay. The houses in whose favour such grants were made and

[1] " And by the practice of the kingdom it became clear law (as it remains also at this day) that regularly, if no other title or discharge to be specially pleaded or shewed in the allegation of the defendant, might appear, every parson had a *common right* to the tithes of all annual increase (prædial and mixt) accruing within the limits of his parish, without showing other title to them in his Libell. That appears frequently in our year books, where the issues taken upon parochial limits are reported." Selden, chap. x. sect. 2, p. 285.

[2] " In 23 Henry II., upon a controversy arising about some tithes challenged by the Priory (of Canterbury) a confirmation was given by Richard, Archbishop of Canterbury, in which he grounds their right upon the deed of the granters. " Cognito " (are his words) "jure prædictorum Monachorum *per inspectionem instrumentorum suorum* considerata etiam diuturna illorum possessione," &c. Selden, chap. xi. sect. 1, p. 318.

formally conveyed were monasteries, convents, abbacies, priories, cells, hospitals, collegiate churches, and capitular establishments. The objects for which they were made were also various. Commonly, the grant was for the use of the poor.[1] Often for the performance of so many masses for the souls of the donors, and of their living and departed relatives.[2] Occasionally it was assigned to the maintenance of an additional monk [3]— or to supply apparel to nuns.[4] Many were the instances in which tithes of English parishes were devoted to monastic institutions beyond the seas.[5] Landlords freely pledged themselves for their tenants' and servants' tithes [6] — promised the legal quota not only for lands under cultivation, but for those to be thereafter brought under cultivation[7]— not only for lands then possessed, but for lands thereafter to be acquired.[8] Some gave their tithes of what-

---

[1] "Et per manus eleemosynarii earum, *in usum pauperum* distribuendam." From the Chartulary of the Monastery of St. Andrew's of Rochester.

[2] "Et ut *missa* pro anima mea, et uxoris meæ, et pro animabus patris et matris meæ, et antecessorum meorum, in prædicta Ecclesia de Boxgrave, ter in unaquaque septimana celebretur." Chartulary of the Priory of Boxgrave in Sussex.

[3] Ibid.

[4] Ledger Book of the Abbey of St. Alban's.

[5] "For a church in one kingdom was often appropriated to a monastery in another." Selden, chap. xii. sect. 1, p. 371.

[6] See above, note 2, p. 66.

[7] Richard of Dodeford gives perpetual right in tithes "de assarto bosci mei de Hecholthe, *cum assartatur et excultus fuerit* sive ego, sive alius per me, illum assartaverit et excoluerit." Chartulary of the Abbey of Osney.

[8] Ralph, Archbishop of Canterbury, gives, "Totam Decimam de meo Dominico, et omnes Decimas omnium villanorum qui habent terram in Dunc, necnon et aliarum omnium, quorum Decimæ meo tempore adquisitæ sunt, vel quocunque tempore adquirentur." Chartulary of St. Andrew's, Rochester.

ever was customarily titheable[1] — some specified the particular kind of tithe, whether of calves, pigs, foals, fleece, cheese, or other things they chose to assign[2] — a few gave tithe of their rents,[3] or the profits of their mills[4] — and not a few arbitrarily conveyed only two parts, or three parts of their tithes.[5] The monks, however, seldom relied upon a single deed, however distinctly that deed might grant away the property of heirs and successors. They generally prevailed upon the heirs, on their succession to their estate, to confirm the grant — they hastened also to obtain the express sanction of either the Pope or the bishop of the diocese, — and they seldom looked upon their property as secure to them until after forty years possession.[6] To complete the information here put before the reader, we subjoin a single specimen of one of these old deeds of tithe conveyance:

"I, Robert Waste, have granted to God, and to Holy Mary of Bec and St. Neots the Confessor, and to his Church of Ernelesbury, and to the monks who serve therein, two parts of my tithe over all my

---

[1] "Quæ decimari solent" or "debent" is the common expression.

[2] Thus, Turold of Harmey grants "Decimam omnium suarum possessionum, *porcellorum, scilicet, agnorum, vellerum.*" Chartulary of the Abbey of Abingdon.

[3] William St. John grants among tithe of other things "Decimam gabulorum de Stretinton, videlicet, *viii. solidos per annum.*" Chartulary of Boxgrave, Sussex.

[4] Peter of Brus, grants "Decimas *molendinorum suorum* in Parochis suis existentium in perpetuum." Ledger Book of the Priory of Gisburne.

[5] "So one Jocelin and his son Randall granted to the Abbey (of Abingdon) two parts of all kinds of tithes in " possessione quadam quæ Grava dicitur." Selden, chap. xi. sect. 1, p. 304.

[6] A large number of the grants set forth by Selden are merely confirmations by successors of grants made by former owners, or by ecclesiastical authority.

estate in Wereslay, of corn and animals of which it is customary to pay tithe — and this is done especially for the soul of Sœnus of Essessa, and for the salvation of my Lord Robert, son of the aforesaid Sœnus, who gave me this land, and for the salvation of Gonnor his wife, and for my own salvation and that of my wife, and of William, son of Gereus, her father, and for the soul of my father, and my mother, and my brother, and all my friends, and all my ancestors, &c."[1]

We cannot dismiss this portion of our investigation without calling the reader's special attention to three or four remarks necessary to give the specific value of the facts set forth above.

1. It is observable that these arbitrary and special consecrations of tithe by the laity do not in the least affect the compulsory and legal origin of the property thus conveyed. Law had again and again enacted that a tenth of the land's annual produce, and even of a man's industrial gains, was due to the Church — and, to some extent, at least, the Church and the State had succeeded in enforcing the claim. Laymen, then, when specially assigning their tithes, were only designating what should be the particular disposition of property which, as to right of enjoyment, the ecclesiastical and civil powers had already forbidden them to regard as their own. They *must* pay tithes, whether they would or no — the only voluntary feature of the transaction was their choice, within certain limits, of the ecclesiastical parties to

---

[1] Chartulary of St. Neots, Huntingdonshire.

whom, and purposes for which, they preferred to pay them. This is a very different thing from individual liberality — in fact it is only a modification of compulsion effected, for a time, by laymens' antagonism to the force brought to bear upon them.[1]

2. It is to be noted distinctly that these grants of tithe by deed of gift, were never grants of parochial tithe *to* the parish Church, but *from* it. They were not settlements, so far as the parish churches were concerned, but *alienations*. No deed can be produced in which a lord of the manor gave the tithe of his estate to the Church which he had founded. It was wholly unnecessary. As soon as the church had received consecration custom assigned some portion of the parish tithe to the maintenance of it and the clergyman — and what that portion should be, the patron could himself determine at each vacancy. But unless he had, by legal transfer, assigned any part of it to other uses, the ground-right to the usufruct, if we may so say, belonged to the parish church *by law*. It was only when such right was interfered with that a legal instrument of conveyance became essential. So that these charters, by which patrons took to themselves the liberty to convey their tithes to ecclesiastical institutions *out* of the parish, instead of being received as evidence of the mode in which parish churches became endowed, may be rather taken as proof that they never were endowed by any such process. "Had the right of tithes," Prideaux sensibly remarks, "grown up

---

[1] Prideaux's "Original and Right of Tithes," chap. v. from p. 191 to p. 199.

from such arbitrary consecrations, as Mr. Selden asserts, why among all his instances does he not bring as much as *one* of such a consecration of tithes in the parish, made to the parish church? Is it likely that those who had such tithes in their power should grant them all from their parish church, and none to it?" And, again, "we may be assured that there was a certain right to these tithes settled *by law* in the parochial churches, before either greedy monk or sacrilegious layman would desire to have them from them, for without such a certain right whereon they could demand, sue for, and recover them by law, they would have been of no use or benefit to them. . . . . For no more was then given them than what was in the parochial churches before."[1] We see, then, that *neither was the tithe property thus conveyed, by deed the original setting apart "to God and the Church" by an act of lay beneficence, nor even if it had been, did any of our parish churches thus become possessed of their endowments.*

3. We now go on to remark that nearly the whole of the tithes assigned by special grant to religious houses subsequently fell into the hands of laymen, through the Acts 27 Henry VIII. cap. 28; and 31 Henry VIII. cap. 13, commonly called the "Statutes of dissolution." The Legislature therein declared that "the King shall have and enjoy, to him and his heirs for ever, all and singular such monasteries and tithes, in as large and ample manner

---

[1] Prideaux's "Original and Right of Tithes," chap. v. pp. 191—199

as the abbots held them;" and that "they who take them from the King, shall have, and hold, and enjoy the same, and have all such actions, suits, entries, and the like, in like manner, form, and condition as before." The monks having been thus forcibly ousted from their well-feathered nests, the spoil was liberally distributed amongst the lay magnates of that day — whence it comes to pass that so large a proportion of parochial tithes is held by lay impropriators. It is now, to all intents and purposes, private property: as such, it forms no object of our present inquiry. But it is interesting to note that the parochial tithes now in possession of the Church as by law established, clearly originated in public law; and that whatever portion of them was given by lay patrons, in charters, grants, and deeds of gift, constituting the only colourable pretext for saying that tithes had their source in private liberality, is already hopelessly and for ever secularised. All that can be pretended to have sprung out of private lay liberality has long since returned to private proprietorship and lay uses.

4. Although not strictly a part of our present object, it may not be out of place to show what light the foregoing statement throws upon the probable origin of Church-rates. In the commencement of the tithe system, whosoever held the fee of tithe, whether bishop, abbot, parish priest, or patron, held it subject to the burden of maintaining, repairing, and decorating the church of the parish from which the tithes were derived. It is certain that the religious houses very grudgingly and inadequately dis-

charged that obligation. It is all but certain that lay patrons were but too ready to follow that bad example. The dilapidation of churches was a common complaint of the times. It seems natural that the lords of manors who held their tithes in fee, should be the first to call upon their tenants to volunteer the performance of the duty which they had themselves neglected — and we know the almost absolute power which these lords brought to bear upon their tenants in those days. If such were the fact, we may be well assured that the monks, whereever they owned parochial tithes, would hasten to copy so convenient a method of supplementing their own notorious negligence in such matters. The parish priest would not be far behind. For the space of two hundred years or more, darkness envelopes the whole affair, and there then emerges into light a common custom, having the force of prescription, for the inhabitants of the parish to rate themselves for the repair of the nave of the church, and for the recipient of the tithes to be responsible for the chancel. Historical facts have not come down to us in sufficient number or variety to authorise our stating the precise manner in which the custom originated, spread, and became binding. We can only guess at that from our knowledge of the forces that were then brought to bear upon ignorant and superstitious minds. No legislative enactment, no canon law, no continental analogy, is in existence to guide our decision. We may fairly conclude that tenants would not spontaneously relieve the tithe-owner of this part of his obligation, but in obedience to some pressure from without. We think it most consistent with all the circumstances of the case, that lords of manors who held the tithes of their parishes in fee, and who were thereby under customary obligation to maintain the churches they had erected, were the first to apply that pressure to their own tenants, on the plea that they had already subjected themselves to the expense of the erection. The example would soon be cited and enforced by the tithe-owning monks. Forty years' prescription would turn a voluntary offering into a legal claim; and thus we, at this day, are saddled with a burden which, during the dark ages, was fraudulently shifted from the owners to the payers of ecclesiastical tithes.

CHAP. VIII.

CONDITIONS OF USUFRUCT PRESCRIBED BY LAW.

Having traced parochial endowments to their origin in *public law* — the authoritative will of the State of the then existing age,— we come now to inquire how it has happened that the property which we know to have been set apart for the support of a church which owned spiritual allegiance to the Pope of Rome, is enjoyed by a church which abjures it. The Church of England as she now is (meaning thereby the somewhat larger half of the population which accepts the Book of Common Prayer, the Thirty-nine Articles, the ecclesiastical organisation, and the Rubric, which the Imperial Legislature have sanctioned) claims to hold precisely the same relation to the endowments originally set apart by the State for pious uses, as was heretofore held by the Church of England as she was before the Reformation.[1] We

---

[1] More than half the mistakes which are made in reference to this subject arise from the widely different meanings attached to the designation, " Church of England." The Protestant Episcopalian community are in the habit of speaking of it as "*our* Church," as if their *legal* and *equitable* relations to it were peculiar and exclusive, whereas it is only their *religious* relation to it that differs from that of the rest of the nation. "The Church of England," they say, " since the Reformation, only differs from the Church of England before the Reformation, as a man may be said to be a different man after he has washed himself." Now, this is

allow that claim. Nay, more, we insist upon it. The Church of England, whether Popish or Protestant, never held any property *absolutely*, and *in her own right* — that is to say, the Civil Power which ordered the setting aside of a certain portion of every man's annual increase for ecclesiastical uses, never surrendered its right to prescribe the conditions which should be attached to the usufruct. The Church always held *from* the State and *subject to* the State. In the palmiest days of papal ascendancy, it is true, ecclesiastics put forth pretensions of the most self-exalting and independent character — and to these lofty pretensions, the Civil Power more than once succumbed under *duresse* — but these occasional triumphs of the ecclesiastical order no more affected *the tenure* by which the Church held her endowments than would a repudiation by a tenant of his landlord's proprietary rights.

When Henry VIII. suppressed the monasteries under the weight of which the kingdom had long groaned, whatever may be thought of the policy of his act, and widely as opinions may vary as to his mode of doing it, it is, at least, historically certain that neither he, nor his Parliament, usurped

---

quite true, but then it is *not* true of the Church of England, if by that term is meant the Protestant Episcopalian body. If true of the Church of England regarded as a body of *persons*, the meaning is that this nation, eccesiastically looked at, is the same nation, ecclesiastically, since, as it was before, the Reformation. But in a legal and constitutional regard, the Church of England is not a community of persons at all, but a system of ecclesiastical rule to which is annexed the property which the state has set apart for ecclesiastical uses. " *The Church*," says Burns in his article under that term, and quoting Gibson for his authority, "*in consideration of law, being, properly,* THE CURE OF SOULS, *and* THE RIGHT OF TITHES," vol. i. p. 321.

any *new* authority. The thing had been done before, though upon a smaller scale, and perhaps, with a different purpose.¹ When, therefore, in the preamble to the statute 27 Henry VIII. cap. 28, it is said: " Whereupon, the said Lords and Commons, by a great deliberation, finally be resolved that it is and shall be much more to the pleasure of Almighty God, and for the honour of this his realm, that the possessions of such small religious houses, now being spent, spoiled and wasted for increase and maintenance of sin, should be used and committed to better uses," the Civil Power (be the motive by which it was guided whatever it might) did but put forth the same sovereign authority, as it had exercised in earlier times, in commanding tithes to be paid by every man "to God and the Church." It had the same right to ordain, as indeed it did (32 Henry VIII. cap. 7), that the proprietor of any " ecclesiastical or spiritual profit which now be, *or which hereafter shall be, made temporal*, or admitted to be,

---

¹ The Templars were suppressed in A.D. 1312, and eleven years afterwards, their lands, churches, advowsons and liberties in England were given by act of Parliament (17 Edward II. s. 3) to the prior and brethren of the hospital of St. John of Jerusalem. About A.D. 1441, Henry VI. dissolved several alien priories, and with their revenues endowed Eton, and King's College, Cambridge. Cardinal Wolsey, by licence of the king and of the pope, obtained a dissolution of above thirty religious houses for the founding and endowing his colleges at Oxford and Ipswich. On the several statutes of dissolution passed during the reign of Henry VIII., Burn, in his "Ecclesiastical Law," makes this pregnant remark: "Upon the whole, it is observable, that the dissolution of these houses was an act, not of the Church, but of the State, prior to the Reformation, by a king and parliament of the Roman Catholic communion, in almost all points except the king's supremacy, and the pope by his bulls and licences had showed the way before."

abide, and go to, or in, temporal hands, and *lay uses and profits*, by the law or statutes of this realm," should, if wrongfully dispossessed, have recovery in the temporal courts, as it had the right to ordain any other appropriation of tithe property.[1] The authority thus exercised for *the secularisation* of what is designated Church property, may have been wisely or unwisely put forth in this particular instance, but it was no newly assumed authority. The State had originally said : " This property shall be devoted to such and such uses " — the State had uniformly, from time to time, laid down the conditions on which it should be enjoyed — and the State, when it saw fit, resumed the property for other uses. The Civil Power, so to speak, never ceased to be lord of the ecclesiastical manor — never parted with the fee simple of the rights it had created.

We catch a glimpse of this constitutional fact in the immemorial provision that the tithes of extra

---

[1] The Statutes of Dissolution are first, 27 Henry VIII. cap. 28, by which about 380 houses were dissolved. They were " small abbeys, priories, and other religious houses of monks, canons, and nuns, where the congregation of religious persons is under the number of twelve persons "— second, 31 Henry VIII. cap. 13, which dealt with the larger monasteries, in consequence of the unsuccessful rebellion occasioned by the first dissolution. By this act no houses were suppressed, but all the surrenders which either were made, or should be made, were confirmed. The third was 32 Henry VIII. cap. 24 which suppressed the Knights of St. John of Jerusalem. The fourth was 37 Henry VIII. cap. 4, which dissolved colleges, free chapels, chantries, hospitals, fraternities, brotherhoods, guilds, &c." The fifth was 1 Edward VI. cap. 14, which vested in the king, his heirs, and successors, " all manner of colleges, free chapels, and chantries, which were not in the actual possession of the late king nor of the king that now is." About a third of the ecclesiastical property of the realm was resumed by the State by means of these acts, and was, for the most part, " made temporal," or converted " to lay uses and profits."

parochial places were due, not to the Church, but to the Crown.[1] It is dimly shadowed forth by the fact that "books of the yearly value of all the spiritual possessions of this realm" were kept "in the king's exchequer,"[2] and still more distinctly by the law which annexed to the Crown the first fruits and tenths of all spiritual dignities, benefices, offices or promotions.[3] We know that in Saxon times, law processes for the recovery of tithes were settled in Courts wherein the *sheriff* sat jointly with the bishop.[4] Selden tells us that "the right of advowson and patronage of churches and tithes only belongs, by our ancient law, and at this day, to the *secular* court."[5] Down to the present time, when-

---

[1] "The tithes of lands which, upon the formation of parishes, were not united to any parish, and which are commonly denominated extra-parochial places, are universally payable to the king in right of his crown, or to persons deriving their titles under grants from the crown."—Eagle on Tithes, chap. iii. sect. 5. And this, be it remembered, was settled law in this country centuries before the sovereign became head of the Church, showing that the seed-plot, as it were, of the tithe system was always held by the State, and not the Church.

[2] "And forasmuch as the clear yearly value of all the said monasteries, and other religious houses in this realm, is certified in the king's exchequer, amongst the books of the yearly valuation of all the spiritual possessions of this realm," &c. Preamble to the fifth clause of 27 Henry VIII. cap. 28.

[3] "Every person before any actual or real possession, or meddling with the profits of his benefice, shall pay, or compound for, the first fruits to the king's use." 26 Henry VIII. cap. 3, s. 2.

[4] "In the Saxon times, a jurisdiction of ecclesiastic causes (among which you may reckon that of tithes, although not much sign of it, in exacting payment of them, appears in the muniments of that age), was exercised jointly by the bishop of the diocese and by the sheriff or alderman of the hundred or county court, where they both sat, the one to judge according to the laws of the kingdom, the other to direct according to divinity." Selden, chap. xiv. sect. 1, p. 412; and he refers for his authority to Leg. Ethelstani, apud Fox in Eccles. Hist. lib. iii. p. 135.

[5] Selden, chap xiv. sect. 3.

ever an inferior court, whether ecclesiastical or civil exceeds the limits of the jurisdiction prescribed for it by the laws and statutes of the realm, in any suit affecting tithes, the Queen's Bench or Common Pleas may issue " a writ of prohibition, " commanding it to cease from the prosecution of such suit.[1] It was by statute (15 Richard II. cap. 6) that in all licenses of appropriation of parish churches, the diocesan was enjoined to take care that vicars should be sufficiently endowed, and " a convenient sum of money be paid and distributed yearly, of the fruits and profits " of such churches " to the poor parishioners . . . in aid of their living and sustenance for ever." It was by statute that some restriction was placed upon pluralities (21 Henry VIII. cap. 13), that the execution of papal bulls was forbidden (2 Henry IV. cap. 4, and 28 Henry VIII. cap. 16), that "no canons, constitutions or ordinances shall be made or put in execution within this realm by authority of the convocation of the clergy which shall be contrary or repugnant to the king's prerogative royal, or the customs, laws, or statutes of this realm." (25 Henry VIII. cap. 19.) In fine, without wearying the reader with details, it appears that from the period of the institution of the tithe system in England, the Civil Power, by de-

[1] That this is no mere modern practice is clear enough from the fact adverted to by Selden, that in the twenty-first year of the reign of Henry II. a national synod of the clergy of England, held at London under Otho, the pope's legate, prayed redress to the effect that, " secular judges should not decide ecclesiastical suits in the temporal courts, such as whether tithes are to be paid of quarries, woods," &c, "which shows," says Selden, "that the temporal courts also, in these elder times, determined what was titheable or not, and so made prohibitions *de non decimando.*"

claring what was and what was not titheable, by taking the rights of patrons under its own protective jurisdiction, by claiming and receiving homage from the higher Church dignitaries for their temporalities[1], by regulating from time to time the uses to which tithes should be appropriated, and by asserting and maintaining the supremacy of its own Courts over every Ecclesiastical Court in the kingdom, especially in all questions relating to title to tithe property, never ceased to assert its determination to withhold from ecclesiastics that which they were ever striving to maintain — *an absolute right* in the endowments created for them by the State.

Thus much for the times preceding the Reformation. Down to that period, assuredly, there was no organised spiritual community which could claim *as its own* the aggregate of Church Property then existing.[2] The law had assigned a certain portion

---

[1] " Whereupon the bishop being introduced into the king's presence, shall do his homage for his temporalities or barony ; by kneeling down and putting his hands between the hands of the king, sitting in his chair of state, and by taking a solemn oath to be true and faithful to his Majesty, and that he holds his temporalities of him. Burn's " Eccles. Law," art. " Bishops," vol. i. p. 211, edit. Phillimore, 1842.

[2] In a very concise and ably written letter to Lord John Russell, and the other Metropolitan Members of Parliament, published in 1852 by Effingham Wilson, under the title of " The Church ; Church Property ; Church Rates ;" there is a very clear and incontestable statement to this effect. The writer says, and every lawyer will bear him out in saying it, " But though the Church in every parish has a common fund, there is no community between the property of one parish and the property of another. Every parish, in respect to its common property, is as distinct and separate from any other parish as the Corporation of London is from the Corporation of Bristol ; there is a community of faith and discipline, but no community of temporal goods in the Church of England. Every parson administers the funds of his own parish. There is no aggregation of these separate funds into a common stock—no division of spoil among Churchmen of different parishes. Every clergyman collects

of the property of every subject to his parochial minister — had permitted certain estates to be set apart for each of the archbishops and bishops and for each dean and chapter. But the law never recognised any right in this kind of revenue beyond the personal or official right of the individual enjoying the usufruct in each case. Every dignitary and parochial parson held his endowments on the freest tenure for his life — but all the dignitaries and parsons put together could not deal with the sum total of their endowments, could not alter their distribution, could not vary the mode of their application, could exercise no one function of a corporate body. The State never would allow such an *imperium in imperio* to be endowed — always jealously guarded against it. Hence, it never gave the Church any corporate rights in, nor any corporate control over, the aggregate of endowments possessed by its clergy — but made every bishop and parochial incumbent a corporation sole, with unrestricted title to the usufruct of his endowments.[1] The lord of the property, in a word, never parted with his lordship.

---

the church revenue of his own parish, and expends what he has thus received." "What has been said of the parson or parish priest, is equally true of bishops and deans."

[1] "The law, therefore, has wisely ordained that the parson, *quatenus* parson, shall never die any more than the sovereign; by making him and his successors a corporation. By which means all the original rights of the parsonage are preserved entire to the successor; for the present incumbent and his predecessor who lived seven centuries ago, are in law, one and the same person; and what was given to the one was given to the other." Blackstone's "Commentaries," book i. chap. xviii. But every parson, *quatenus* parson, is independent of every other parson, and no two parsons, nor any number whatever of parsons, form a corporation aggregate.

Accordingly, at the period of the Reformation, there was no transference of these endowments from one spiritual corporation to another. Indeed, it is quite instructive to observe how utterly the Legislature ignored the idea that there was besides itself any claimant to the property. It knew nothing of the Church save as a national institution, maintained from sources which itself had opened, over which it had watchfully kept guard, and some of which it had entirely diverted. It set about the work of reformation with as much freedom as the War Office at this day would set about remodelling the army, or the Admiralty reconstructing the navy. The only way in which it touched the property question was to secularise a considerable portion of it, and to impose afresh the obligation of tithes upon all subjects. That done, the king assigned to a commission the task of drawing up a new liturgical service, which it enjoined every clergyman to use, and new articles of faith which it commanded every clergyman to subscribe and read in his parish church.[1] In the second year of Edward VI.'s reign,

---

[1] Down to the end of Henry VIII.'s reign, the Latin services of the Church of Rome were used in all the English churches. In the second year of Edward VI. an Act was passed, the preamble of which sets forth that the king had "appointed the Archbishop of Canterbury, and certain other of the most learned and discreet bishops and other learned men of this realm," "to draw and make one convenient and meet order, rite, and fashion of common and open prayer and administration of the sacraments," "the which, by the aid of the Holy Ghost, with one uniform agreement is of them concluded, set forth, and delivered in a book, entitled 'The Book of Common Prayer and Administration of the Sacraments, and other Rites and Ceremonies of the Church, after the use of the Church of England;'" whereupon the Lords Spiritual and Temporal and the Commons in Parliament assembled, "pray that it may be enacted

the present form (in all substantial particulars) of consecrating and ordaining bishops, priests, and deacons was established. By the 3 and 4 Edward VI. cap. 10, s. 1, it was enacted that "all books heretofore used for the service of the Church, other than such as shall be set forth by the King's Majesty, shall be clearly abolished." By 5 and 6 Edward VI. cap. 1, it is enacted—"The King, with the assent of the Lords and Commons in Parliament, hath annexed the Book of Common Prayer to this present statute." All these ecclesiastical changes, as is well known, were subverted by Queen Mary (except the secularisation of property) and restored by Elizabeth[1], and most of the bishops and clergy, in each instance, conformed to them.

by his Majesty, that all and singular ministers in any cathedral or parish church, or other place within this realm, shall be bounden to say and use the matins, evensong, celebration of the Lord's Supper, commonly called the mass, and administration of each the sacraments, and all their common and open prayer, in such order and form as is mentioned in the same book, and none other, or otherwise." The penalty of disobedience was "for his first offence, he shall forfeit to the king the profit of such one of his spiritual benefices or promotions as it shall please the king to appoint, coming or arising in one whole year after his conviction, and also be imprisoned for six months; and for his second offence be imprisoned for a year, and be deprived *ipso facto* of all his spiritual promotions, and the patron shall present to the same as if he were dead; and for the third offence shall be imprisoned during life; and if he shall not have any spiritual promotion, he shall for the first offence suffer imprisonment six months, and for the second offence imprisonment during life." The Thirty-nine Articles were mainly founded upon a body of articles compiled and published in the reign of King Edward VI.

[1] The Thirty-nine Articles passed in Convocation, and confirmed by royal authority in 1562, were ratified anew in 1571, in the following form. "This book of articles before rehearsed is again approved, and allowed to be holden and executed within the realm, by the assent and consent of our Sovereign Lady, Elizabeth." By the 13 Eliz. cap. 12, "none shall be admitted to the order of deacon, unless he shall first subscribe to the said articles,"—"no person shall be admitted to any benefice

This bare historical outline (and it is nothing more) may serve to show how devoid of all foundation is the pretence of Conformists that the endowments of the Church of England are so exclusively *their own* that the Legislature could not withdraw them without incurring the guilt of spoliation and sacrilege. National authority created these endowments, and annexed them, not to a spiritual community of persons, but to a special plan of ecclesiastical order, discipline, faith, and service, which the same authority changed whenever it saw fit.[1] The relation of the property to *persons* was never entertained but only to *things*. The State uniformly prescribed the conditions on which the usufruct should depend. It did not hand over the fee simple to a religious body who had conformed to its will — but it required conformity as a preceding condition to enjoyment — nor did it enter into compact with a previously existing spiritual organisation having independent rights, but, in the case of the Church of England as it now is, it actually *constituted*

---

with cure, except he shall first have subscribed," &c.; and lastly, "if any person ecclesiastical, or which shall have ecclesiastical living, shall advisably maintain or affirm any doctrine directly contrary or repugnant to any of the said Articles, and being convened before the bishop of the diocese, or the ordinary, shall persist therein, or not revoke his error, or after such revocation, eftsoons affirm such untrue doctrine, he shall, by such bishop or ordinary, be deprived of his ecclesiastical promotions."

[1] We have not noted in the text *all* the changes which the Legislature has made in the conditions on which ecclesiastical endowments should be held. There was the change from Protestant Episcopalianism as established by Elizabeth, to Presbyterianism as established by the Commonwealth; and the return to the government by bishops, priests, and deacons, the Thirty-nine Articles, and the Book of Common Prayer, under Charles II., with a third Act of Uniformity, and a St. Bartholomew's Day.

the organisation, and applied the separate fund which it had anciently created, and never surrendered, to its support.¹ As supreme lord, and absolute owner, it simply prescribed and enforced new conditions of trust.

[1] Nothing, as the foregoing notes will show, could be more summary or arbitrary than the mode in which the Legislature has been accustomed to deal with the usufructuaries of Church endowments. It has wholly deprived them when it saw fit, as it did when it passed the Statutes of Dissolution. It has changed all the conditions on which they held them, and all their religious professions and duties five times over. It never allowed the smallest compensation to objectors, but punished them severely for disobedience. In a word, it has uniformly proceeded on the assumption that the fee of Church property is in the State, and that it belongs to the State to prescribe the service to be rendered by those whom it puts in possession of it.

CHAP. IX.

GENERAL CONCLUSIONS.

GATHERING up the conclusions which we take to have been fairly established in the foregoing chapters, we think they may be expressed to the following effect.

1. The Church of England, viewed in any such light as will warrant one part of the nation in calling it *their* Church, in a sense, at least, in which it is not equally the Church of every other subject of the realm, is nothing more than a *system* of ecclesiastical faith, government, usage, and service, " as established by law." As Metternich called Italy " a geographical expression," so the Church of England may be described as " a politico-ecclesiastical expression." The British Constitution knows nothing of it as a body distinguishable from the whole people.[1] It

---

[1] " We hold that, seeing there is not any man of the Church of England but the same man is also a member of Commonwealth, nor any member of the Commonwealth which is not also of the Church of England; therefore, as in a figure triangle, the base doth differ from the sides thereof, and yet one and the self-same line is both a base and also a side; a side simply, a base if it chance to be the bottom and underlie the rest; so, albeit, properties and actions of one do cause the name of a commonwealth, qualities and functions of another sort, the name of a church — yet one and the self-same multitude may in such sort be both. Nay, it is so with us, that no person appertaining to the one can be denied also to be of the other."—Hooker's " Eccles. Polity." Lord Chancellor Eldon said " he knew no difference, as to the persons of whom they are composed, between the Church and the State,—the Church is the State, and the State is the Church."

knows nothing of it as having rights apart from the whole people. Practically, and in relation to all national ecclesiastical endowments, the Church of England as a corporate unity, does not exist. It is not possible to represent the Church of England in any of our courts of law. It is only by a figure of speech that we talk of the Church as a living entity. She can neither, as such, sue or be sued. She can own no property, and therefore she can be despoiled of none. What our Constitution *does* recognise is what our Parliament itself created—namely, a body of laws regulating the ecclesiastical affairs of this nation, and a number of ecclesiastical officers to whom it entrusts the carrying out those laws, under its supreme authority, in obedience to its prescriptions, and maintained by arrangements, and mainly from sources, which it originally created.

2. The Constitution of this realm, in recognising the claims of the bishops and clergy arising out of their discharge of the duties assigned to them by Parliament, recognises those claims only as they are personal, individual, and separate. A bishop may maintain a legal claim to the revenues assigned to him by Act of Parliament—a dean and chapter may do the same—a rector or vicar may do the same—but the law knows nothing whatever of a common ecclesiastical fund, claimable by an organised and corporate ecclesiastical body. Every official member of the Church of England has *his* rights of property and position, given him by law, as against all other claimants—and the aggregate number of ecclesiastical officials we call, for convenience' sake, the

H

Church, just as we may term the whole body of military men in the service of the State, the Army. But everybody knows that the Army cannot, as a whole, put in a claim for corporate and distinctive rights, nor can it own any property. Every man now in the Army has a moral and equitable claim upon Parliament and the people for a full pecuniary consideration in recompense of his services — but supposing the State should resolve to do away with its military establishment, it would be most absurd to pretend that, after the satisfaction of all personal claims arising out of existing interests, there would be any Army rights violated.[1] Now the Church of England, in respect of any claims it may be supposed to have upon Parliament and the people, differs nothing from the Army, except in the special mode of maintenance provided by law for its officers of every grade. The fact that the law of the realm has set apart for every parochial incumbent a freehold for life, gives *him* a just claim to the undisturbed enjoyment of it—gives some claim, perhaps, to those who are under training for the ecclesiastical office — gives some claim to the patron who has the legal right to present to the office — but supposing all these personal claims liberally satisfied, there remains no other claim to be considered.[2] The Church of England is no more a corporate body than the Army of England.

---

[1] Sir James Macintosh, in the "Vindiciæ Gallicæ," says on this subject: "It would not be less absurd for the priesthood to exercise such authority (viz. that of proprietors) over these lands, than it would be for seamen to claim the property of the fleet they manned, or soldiers that of a fortress they garrisoned."

[2] Lord Brougham, in a speech delivered in 1825, after describing the

3. Neither can the whole number of Protestant Episcopalians have any claim as against the nation. They are in the habit of speaking of the Church of England as "*our*" Church, as if it was an inheritance to which they have a peculiar and exclusive claim. Certainly, it happens to them that the religious polity, the faith, the discipline, the liturgy, the offices, rites and ceremonies, ordained by law, and supported by public endowments, accord with their individual convictions, and in this respect they get more advantage out of the arrangement than those who cannot think and believe as they do. But this does not give them a single right in the Church which other subjects of the realm, whether absenters or dissenters, do not equally possess. The Church was framed by Parliament for the whole people — not for a part of them — and it is curious doctrine that those who cannot appropriate its benefits lose their title to any share of the inheritance. Surely, it is misfortune enough to be deprived of the advantage of an ecclesiastical common, provided

---

essential elements of private property, thus contrasts with them those of Church endowments. "How does the property of the parson at all correspond with this description? He can neither sell it nor transfer it, nor leave it to whom he pleases; but it passes from him to a successor of whom he knows nothing, and who, perhaps, has been his mortal enemy. If private property were to be taken from an individual, the State would rob, not only him but his children or next heirs; but if the law says to a clerical incumbent, 'the profits of this living shall cease after your death,' who in whom that clergyman has any interest is in the smallest degree damnified? Besides, is it not clear that private property is that income for the receipt of which the holder has no duty to perform? The clergy are officers of the State, and, like other officers of the State, may be got rid of in proportion as they are no further wanted."—*Mirror of Parliament*, 1825, p. 367.

by and for the public, whether because we have no cattle to graze there, or because we prefer feeding our flocks and herds in inclosed meadows — and it is "adding insult to injury" to tell us that by ceasing to use our privilege, we lose our rights. Happily, this is not constitutional law — for, in the eye of law, the Church of England is, in relation to the rights of the subject, no more the inheritance of one man than of another — no more of the Protestant Episcopalians than of other religious bodies.

4. Neither can Protestant Episcopalian*ism*, as an ecclesiastical polity, put in any special or independent claim to the use of Church property in these realms. It never existed in this country, at least in an embodied shape,' but as the result of parliamentary decision. It did not come to the State with endowments of its own. In point of fact, it not only did not possess prior rights, but it had not even a prior existence. It was King, Lords, and Commons that begat Protestant Episcopalianism, and then bade Roman Catholicism turn out and make room for it. Queen, Lords, and Commons, shortly afterwards, quite as unceremoniously ousted it, and reinstated Romanism. A second time it was installed by Elizabeth and her Parliament — then had to turn out, under the Commonwealth, for Presbyterianism — and a third and last time was exalted by Charles II. and the Legislature of his day. But the endowments did not follow Protestant Episcopalianism. They remained with the *State*-Church, whether Roman, Episcopalian, or Presbyterian — and for the simple reason that the

State always retained the absolute right of the endowments which, for the most part, its own laws had called into existence.

5. After what we have already written, we hope it will be beyond all doubt that our whole system of parochial Church endowments originated in public law. We have proved this by producing the successive laws, extending over a period of three centuries, by which those endowments were created — laws which were sharply enforced, and not very willingly obeyed. We have found it in the nature of those endowments, in the articles of annual increase out of which they accrued, in the legal principles which governed their measurement and appropriation, and in the uniformity and universality of their occurrence. We have witnessed the growth of by far the greater part of them out of the extension and improvement of agriculture since the period of their first institution. And we have seen that any pretence of their having sprung out of private liberality, such as the voluntary charging their estates with this burden by lords of manors, is a gross perversion of a class of historic facts which, examined with attention, prove just the reverse. We have a right, therefore, until our statement is shown to be historically incorrect, to assume as proven the position with which we started—namely, that parochial Church endowments are nothing more nor less than the peculiar provision made by the State to give effect to its ecclesiastical policy for the time being; which policy it has changed as frequently as it has seen fit, and which it is equally entitled, to change

or to suppress altogether, as public opinion shall authorise and require it.

6. For the State has never allowed the fee-simple of Church property to pass from under its own control. It has never given the Church a legislative power over it — never invested her with the rights of ownership. It has itself prescribed all the conditions of usufruct, and, even in respect of the landed estates in the hands of the bishops, it has exacted homage to the Crown, as feudal sovereign, for their possession. In every sense, by every method, through all times, in which the great Council of the nation could declare that Church property is but national property ecclesiastically applied, it has done so. The recent commutation, in our own day, of tithes into rent-charges[1], is the last and crowning act by which the Legislature has asserted its absolute ownership of these endowments. There is no more analogy between these endowments and those which have been conferred by private donation or bequest in modern times, than there is between a public tax and an individual gift. Let us hear no more of the assumption, so gravely put forth of late, that the two are identical in their nature. There has been too much of this practice of solemnly misleading the public. We have charity enough to attribute it to ignorance, as yet. But it will not be our fault if, for the future, any such apology be accepted for this perversion of history.

---

[1] See the Tithe Commutation Act in the Appendix.

SUPPLEMENTARY CHAPTER.

The substance of the text of the foregoing Treatise appeared between two or three years ago in a periodical publication edited by the writer, but under a somewhat different arrangement, in an unrevised shape, and without any reference to the authorities on which its historic facts and legal statements were based. Requests that the series of papers then submitted to the public should be put into a more permanent form were so numerous and pressing, that compliance with them seemed to be a duty. But the motives of the author in preparing this volume were quickened by the mode in which the subject to which it relates has been pretty uniformly treated by the clergymen and laymen who have recently lectured in various parts of the country on behalf of Church Defence Associations. Believing that the unfounded allegations which, with a unanimity truly wonderful, these gentlemen have confidently made, with regard to the nature and origin of the great bulk of Church property, must have been adopted in entire ignorance of the facts of the case, the author compiled the present Treatise in the hope that it may be of use in correcting those views of the question which, however often reiterated, have no foundation whatever in history. It certainly seems desirable that, on a matter purely historical or legal, reliable information should be the groundwork of all positive assertions and the purpose kept in view throughout this work has been to substitute reliable information for mistakes of the fancy.

One main cause of misapprehension, on the subject discussed in the foregoing pages, seems to have been the unreflecting habit of putting into one and the same category all the various kinds of property enjoyed by the Established Church, and tracing them up to the same source. It is true, no doubt, that many of the landed estates in the possession of the Church were the donations or bequests of individual proprietors, and were the whole truth ascertainable, it would doubtless be found that they were originally bestowed with annexed conditions which are no longer legal. But the parochial endowments formerly known by the name of tithes, and now commuted into rent-charges, comprehending by far the largest proportion of Church property, ought not to be confounded with the lands given to the Church, as though the mode in which they were acquired were in both instances the same. "He that talks of tithes," says the learned Selden, "without reference to such positive law, makes the object of his discourse rather what he would have it to be, than anything that indeed is at all. For what state is in all Christendom wherein tithes are paid *de facto*, otherwise than according to human law positive? that is, is subject to some customs, to statutes, to all civil disposition? What colour could they have had to think that they had been only alms? for whatever is lawfully established by a civil title, is clearly *debitum justitiæ*, not *charitatis*."[1]

Another fertile cause of misapprehension in relation to this subject is the assumption that the Church of England is a corporate body. Even prelates in their visitation charges have spoken of it as such, without appearing to be aware that they were "drawing upon their imagination for their facts." It is extremely easy, and even natural, to take for granted that there must be a collective body, or, as it has been designated by the Bishop of Salisbury, "an ecclesiastical corporation," to which so large an amount of property separately belongs, — easy, because so many existing municipal corporations suggest as well as illustrate the idea, and natural, because in the present state of society in this kingdom, where the Church Establishment is surrounded by various denominations of Dissenters, it would seem, at first sight, that the property appropriated to the former must be held by her in some such form as will exclude the latter from an equal right of participation. But, however easy and natural the misconception may be, it *is* a misconception, and it is one that gives rise to many theoretical mistakes, and apparent justification to much practical injustice. It would be to the credit of Churchmen, lay as well as clerical, in parliament as well as in the cathedral, to revise some of the phrases which they are in the habit of using, and where they are found to be significant of no corresponding reality, to dismiss them as tending to make false impressions. The phrase "ecclesiastical corpo-

---

[1] "History of Tithes," Pref. pp. xiv. xv.

ration," when applied to the Church of England, is one of this misleading character. In the "Edinburgh Review" for January 1835 (p. 487), the fallacy suggested by the phrase is thus pointed out:—

"The term 'Church' includes the laity as well as the clergy; and it is plain that in this sense it cannot be a corporate body. But neither is it a corporate body if it is understood to comprise only the clergy. The clergy, collectively, are not a corporation, any more than the laity are a corporation. If they are distinct, so are the laity—if they are privileged, so are the nobility; but they have, like them, no collective corporate existence."

Lord Brougham, in a speech delivered in the House of Lords in 1833 on the Irish Church Temporalities Bill, is still more emphatic. He said,—

"He had yet to learn that this Church was in any sense of the word to be regarded as a corporation. The Church had not the least similitude to a corporation,—it had not a single one of the incidents of a corporation annexed to it; in fact, the idea of the Church was utterly incompatible with the idea of a corporation."

A third cause of misapprehension on the subject that has been discussed in this Treatise is the entirely unfounded view which the clergy generally take of their own position. Their office is sacred, and, as religious men, they owe primary allegiance to the Divine Head of the Church. The temporalities by which they are sustained are held by a tenure which, in effect, leaves them all but irresponsible to the State. Under these circumstances, they are apt to look upon themselves as an independent body, and upon the property set apart for their maintenance as rightfully their own. It is not often that any event occurs to remind them of the true nature of their relationship to the State. The great majority of them, it is probable, pass through life without the smallest consciousness that their religious services are as due to, and are as much under the control of, the State, as is the military service of every officer in the army, and that, although their occupation is very different, their proceedings less interfered with, and their remuneration less direct and more assured, their relation to the civil power is precisely the same. On this point they might do well to ponder seriously the words of Lord Chancellor Hardwicke, which, in the following quotation from a speech delivered by his Lordship in a debate on the Mortmain Bill, 1736, is printed in italics to attract to it their especial attention. His words are:—

"With respect my lords, to the clergy of the Established Church, I am really sorry to hear that there are so many worthy clergymen of the Established Church struggling with poverty and want, at the same time that they are rendering such services to their country; and I must think it a blemish to our constitution, at least that part of it which is called the Established Church, to have so many of its members living in the greatest poverty and distress, whilst a great number of others are wallowing in the greatest affluence and ease; for since they are *all servants of the public, and are paid by the public*, every man ought to have a proper share of public rewards."

To the causes above alluded to, and to others which it is unnecessary to specify in this place, may be attributed the mistake so generally prevalent amongst the clergy of the Establishment, that the property of the Church is the property of a corporation, and not of the public,— a mistake which historians, lawyers, and statesmen of no mean repute have, within the last thirty years, exposed and condemned. There seems to be, in the present day, such an utter want of acquaintance with what our greatest men have said or written on this subject, or such a complete forgetfulness of it, that no apology is required for reproducing *in extenso* the arguments, statements, and public declarations of several of the most prominent men of our age on this question. The following somewhat lengthy quotations from Sir James Macintosh's "Vindiciæ Gallicæ"[1] are deserving of consideration, and, if his argument be rejected, of an answer:—

"Are the lands occupied by the Church the *property* of its members? Various considerations present themselves which may elucidate the subject.

"1. It has not hitherto been supposed that any class of public servants are proprietors. They are *salaried* by the state for the performance of certain duties. Judges are *paid* for the distribution of justice; kings, for the execution of the laws; soldiers, where there is a mercenary army for public defence; and priests, where there is an established religion for public instruction. The mode of their payment is indifferent to the question. It is generally in rude ages by land, and in cultivated ages by money; but a territorial pension is no more property than a pecuniary one. The right of the state to regulate the salaries of those servants whom it pays in money, has not been disputed. But if it have chosen to provide the revenue of a certain portion of land for the salary of another class of servants, wherefore is its right more disputable to resume that land, and to establish a new mode of payment?

"2. The lands of the Church possess not the most simple

[1] Pp. 85—96.

and indispensable requisites of property. They are not even pretended to be held for the benefit of those who enjoy them. This is the obvious criterion between private property and a pension for public service. The destination of the first is avowedly the comfort and happiness of the individuals who enjoy it; as he is conceived to be the sole judge of this happiness, he possesses the most unlimited rights of enjoyment, alienation, and even abuse. But the lands of the Church destined for the support of public servants, exhibit none of the characters of property. They are inalienable; for it would not be less absurd for the priesthood to exercise such authority over these lands than it would be for seamen to claim the property of a fleet they manned, or soldiers that of a fortress they garrisoned.

" 3. It is confessed that no individual priest is a proprietor, and it is not denied that his utmost claim was limited to a possession for life of his stipend. If all the priests, taken individually are not proprietors, the priesthood, as a body, cannot claim any such right, — for what is a body but an aggregate of individuals, and what new right can be conveyed by a mere change of name? Nothing can so forcibly illustrate this argument as the case of other corporations. They are voluntary associations of men for their own benefit. Every member of them is an absolute sharer in their property. It is therefore alienated and inherited. Corporate property is here as sacred as individual, because in the ultimate analysis it is the same. But the priesthood is a corporation endowed by the country, and destined for the benefit of other men. It is hence that the members have no separate, nor the body any collective, right of property. They are only entrusted with the administration of the lands from which their salaries are paid.

" 4. It is from this last circumstance that their legal semblance of property arises. In charters, bonds, and all other proceedings of law they are treated with the same formalities as real property. The argument of *prescription* will appear to be altogether untenable, for prescription implies a certain period during which the rights of property have been exercised, but in the case before us they never were exercised, because they never could be supposed to exist. It must be proved that these possessions were of the nature of property before it can follow that they are protected by prescription, and to plead it is to take for granted the question in dispute. If they never were property, no length of time can change their nature.

"5. The clamour of sacrilege, by which at the Reformation, the Church attempted to protect its pretended property, seems to have fallen into early contempt. The treaty of Westphalia secularised many of the most opulent benefices in Germany. In our own island, on the abolition of episcopacy in Scotland, the revenues of the Church peaceably devolved on the sovereign. When, at a later period, the Jesuits were suppressed in most Catholic monarchies, the wealth of that formidable and opulent body was everywhere seized by the sovereign. In all these memorable examples, no traces are to be discovered of the pretended property of the Church. The salaries of a class of public servants are, in all these cases, resumed by the State when it ceases to deem their service, or the mode of it, useful.

"6. The whole subject is, indeed, so evident, that little diversity of opinion could have arisen if the question of church-property had not been confounded with the claims if present incumbents. The distinction is extremely simple: the State is the proprietor of the church revenues, but its faith, it may be said, is pledged to those who have entered into the Church for the continuance of their incomes, for which they abandoned all other pursuits. The right of the State to arrange at its pleasure the revenues of any future priests may be confessed, while a doubt may be entertained whether it is competent to change the fortune of those to whom it has solemnly promised a certain income for life."

The opinion of Lord Brougham, quoted in a note to Chapter IX. of the text, page 99, is equally decisive; nor is that of Lord Campbell less unequivocally in the same direction. In his speech on the Irish Church Bill of 1836, he said,—

"When the Christian religion was first planted in this land, it was supported by the voluntary oblations of the faithful; by and by, all were expected to contribute one-tenth of their substance, and to these it became a legal obligation; but, by law, there was a four-fold division, and an alteration, which could only have been made by law, was made, by which the bishops were amply endowed with lands, the clergy got the tithes for their own use, the repairs of the church were left to the parish, and the poor were thrown on charity. The vested rights of individuals are not to be disturbed by resumption or new distribution. This being protected, the appropriation of the property remains with the State by which it was granted. All was subject to the implied condition that the public good requires a change in its destinies; and I hold, that as the grant was made by the State, that the State should superintend its application; it is in the power of the State, without sacrilege or injustice, to reserve any part of this property, and apply it to other purposes when such might tend to the good of religion, and for the public welfare."

Passing now from the opinions of lawyers to those of modern statesmen on this point, the first place, in order of time, is due to Lord Melbourne. The quotation which follows is from a speech delivered by that nobleman in the House of Lords in the debate on the Ecclesiastical Commission in 1837:—

"The tithes and landed property in the hands of clergymen, do not belong to them, but it is a portion of the national property, which has been set aside, either by the institution of the country, or by the superstitions of former ages, for the maintenance of the Established religion of this country; and being a portion of that national property, it is in the power of the State, from time to time, to increase it, should it be too small, or to diminish it, if too large, and apply the surplus to whatever purposes might be considered the fittest to promote the great end and object in view. These are the only safe principles upon which the legislature or government can proceed."

Lord Althorp, in the debate in the House of Commons, May 6th, 1833, on the Irish Church Temporalities Bill, "would not admit that there was any analogy between church-property and that of corporations,—and still less was there any between it and the property of private individuals."

Lord Palmerston has equally committed himself to the opinion maintained in the foregoing extracts. So lately as May 27th, 1856, in a debate in the House of Commons on the Irish Church, he said,—

"I do not go along with those who maintain that the property of the Church strictly belongs to the ministers of religion, and that Parliament cannot deal with it. No doubt the property of the Church belongs to the State, and the State, represented by its proper organ, the legislature, has the power and the right to deal with that property according to the circumstances of the times."

So also Lord Macaulay,—

"His own opinion of church-property was that it was a sort of mixed property — that it was something more than a salary, and something less than an estate; and no man could deny, after the cases he had quoted, that the legislature had a right to deal with it. Parliament had the same power to alter and remand as to frame, and the Church of England had no rights except under the Act of the Legislature."[1]

A passage from the "Edinburgh Review,"[2] traceable, we suspect to the same high authority, may be added to the foregoing. After an elaborate statement of the nature of ecclesiastical property, the reviewer proceeds:—

---

[1] Debate on Irish Ch. Temp. Bill, April 1, 1833.
[2] July 1837, p. 187.

"There is in reality no possibility of avoiding the position that Church property is, to all intents and purposes, public property, a portion of the funds belonging to the State, and over which the legislature has the undoubted right of distribution and division; and has the duty of applying it so as best to answer the ends for which all public property is placed under the control of the legislature, namely, to promote the civil and religious interests of the community. But no distinction can be drawn between this and all the other funds of the State; and the Church is no more a corporation within the State, having a right to the exclusive possession and management of the funds hitherto destined for its support, than the army or the revenue departments of the public service are corporate bodies, entitled to the portion of the public income hitherto appropriated to their sustentation.

If it be true, as the text of the foregoing Treatise sufficiently proves, that what is usually called Church Property — at any rate, all that portion of it which consists in Tithes or Rent Charges — was originally created by Public Law, it will certainly be difficult to resist the conclusion variously set forth in the foregoing extracts that it is National Property. It would appear superfluous to give any further authority for ascribing it to this origin, but as it is a point of supreme importance in this controversy, and as some minds are disposed to give more heed to the statements of clergymen on this subject than to that of lawyers, reviewers, or statesmen, the following passage from Dean Milman's "History of Latin Christianity,"* showing the origin of Tithes in the Western Empire, is appended.

"On the whole body of the clergy, Charlemagne bestowed their even more vast dowry — the legal claim to tithes. Al-

---

* Vol. ii. pp. 292, 293.

ready, under the Merovingians, the clergy had given significant hints that the law of Leviticus was the perpetual and unrepealed law of God. Pepin had commanded the payment of tithes for the celebration of peculiar litanies during a period of famine. Charlemagne made it a law of the empire; he enacted it in its most strict and comprehensive form, as investing the clergy in a right to the tenth of the substance, and of the labour alike of freeman and of serf. The collection of tithe was regulated by compulsory statutes; the clergy took note of all who refused to pay; four, eight, or more jurymen were summoned from each parish, as witnesses for the claims disputed; the contumacious were three times summoned; if still obstinate, excluded from the Church; if they still refused to pay, they were fined, over and above the whole tithe, six solidi; if further contumacious, the recusant's house was shut up; if he attempted to enter it, he was cast into prison, to await the judgment of the next plea of the Crown. The tithe was by no means a spontaneous votive offering of the whole Christian people—it was a tax imposed by imperial authority, enforced by imperial power. It had caused one, if not more than one, sanguinary insurrection among the Saxons. It was submitted to in other parts of the empire not without strong reluctance."

Dean Milman adds in a note to this passage:—

"Even Alcuin ventures to suggest that if the apostles of Christ had demanded tithes, they would not have been so successful in the propagation of the Gospel."

Much to the same effect is the historical judgment of the Rev. J. C. Robertson, vicar of Beakesbourne, as will be seen in the following passages from his History of the Christian Church.*

"But although the policy of Charlemagne did much to spread the proofs of Christianity, the means which he em-

---

* Vol. ii. pp. 131, 191.

ployed were open to serious objection. The enforcement of tithe naturally raised a prejudice against the faith of which this payment was made a condition, and in 793 it produced a revolt of the Saxons. Alcuin often remonstrated against the unwise exaction. He acknowledged the lawfulness of tithes, but how, he asked, would an impost which was ill borne even by persons who had been brought up in the Catholic Church, be endured by a rude and barbarous race of neophytes? Would the apostles have enforced it in such circumstances? When confirmed in the faith, the converts might properly be subjected to such burdens, but until then it would be a grievous error to risk the faith itself for the sake of tithes."

And again:—

"The first canon which required it [the payment of tithes] was passed by the Council of Maçon, in 585. But it would seem that this canon had little effect, and no attempt to re-enforce it was made by the Frankish Councils during the remainder of the Merovingian period. Pepin for the first time added the authority of the secular power to that of the Church for the exaction of tithes; but little was done until the reign of Charlemagne, who by a capitulary of 779 enacted that they should be paid. The payment was enforced, not only by excommunication, but by heavy civil penalties graduated according to the obstinacy of the delinquent; and the obligation was extended to the newly acquired territories beyond the Rhine, where (as we have already seen) it had the effect of exciting a strong prejudice against the Christian faith. . . . The tithe had at first been exacted only for corn. It was then extended to other productions of the soil, such as flax and wine, and in some places to the increase of animals. The enactments of Charlemagne's time usually speak of it as payable on the "whole property." But it was long before the clergy succeeded in establishing a general compliance with their claims in this respect."

Fuller also will be thought worth listening to by

not a few. He thus writes on the origin of Tithes in England:—

" Before his time (Ethelwulph's) many Acts for tithes are produced, which when pressed will prove of no great validity. Such are the imperial edicts in civil law; never possessed of full power in England; as, also, the canons of some councils and popes, never admitted into plenary obedience by the consent of prince and people. Add to these, first, such laws as were made by King Ina and Offa, monarchs, indeed, of England in these times, as I may say, but not devising the same to the issues of their bodies: so that their acts, as personal, may by some froward spirits be cavilled at as determining with their own lives. Join to these (if producible) any provincial constitutions of an English archbishop (perchance, Egbertus of York): those might obey them who would obey, being otherwise not subject to any civil penalty. But now this Act of Ethelwulph's appears entire in all the proportions of a law, made in his great Council, equivalent to after-parliaments, not only *cum consilio episcoporum*, with the advice of his bishops, which easily may be presumed willingly to concur in such a matter of church advancement, but also *principum meorum;* of my princes, saith he, the consent of inferior persons not being required in that age." *

" True it is that this law did not presently find an universal obedience in all the land, and the wonder is not great, if at the first making thereof, it met with many recusants; since, corroborated by eight hundred years' prescription, and many confirmations, it finds obstacles and oppositions at this day."†

Bishop Stillingfleet, more profoundly versed, perhaps, than any man of his time in Ecclesiastical Law, especially in its relations to the Church of England, takes precisely the same view. In his "Duties and

---

* Fuller's "Church History," vol. i. p. 289, Oxford ed. 1845.
† Ibid. p. 293.

Rights of the Parochial Clergy,"* writing on the origin of parishes in this country, he says, incidentally, as it were, and as a fact not to be controverted:

"In the times of Edgar and Canutus, we read of the Mother Churches which had the original settlement of Tithes (after they were given to the Church by several laws)". And again touching the maintenance of the parochial clergy, he writes:—"As to the foundation they (Tithes) stand upon in point of law, my lord Coke not only saith " That the parochial right of Tithes is established by divers Acts of Parliament, but he mentions the Saxon laws before the Conquest for the payment of Tithes, of Edward and Guthrun, Ethelstan, Edmund, Edgar, Canutus and King Edward's confirmed by William I.† And a little further on he sums up in few words:‡ " The settlement of tithes among us has been by ancient and unquestionable laws of the land."

Ayliffe, another high authority amongst churchmen, is quite as decisive on this point. In page 505 of his Parergon, he says: "I shall not here enter into a controversy about the Divine Right of Tithes due to the Clergy, but consider them as given to the Church by human laws for the maintenance of such as serve at the altar." And then, in the next page, he writes: "Doubtless the laws which gave them Tithes, may give them any other portion or substance in lieu of Tithes." Bishop Watson, in a Charge to his Clergy, goes somewhat further than Ayliffe, and seems to give up as untenable the position that

* P. 128.   † Ibid. p. 254.   ‡ Ibid. 276.

Church Property is sacred. These are his words: "The true question is, whether the uses to which it is appropriated are such as an enlightened Government can approve of; for we by no means contend that every appropriation once made, whether beneficial to the community or not, must be perpetuated." The last point is epigrammatically put by Bishop Warburton, in a sentence contained in a note on Clarendon's "History of the Rebellion," referring to the demand of Parliament for the alienation of Church lands. "The State," he observes, "may resume what the State originally gave." We conclude this list of authorities in support of the main conclusion sought to be established by the foregoing Treatise with a sentence from a pamphlet ("The Liturgy and the Dissenters") recently published, in which the writer, a clergyman of the Church of England, the Rev. Isaac Taylor, thus pithily disposes of the whole question herein discussed:—"Her revenues," he says, "for the most part are not private foundations like the endowments of Dissenters, but are national property, and are, and have been controlled by Parliament in a manner which would be utterly inappropriate and unjustifiable in the case of the revenues of any body of Dissenters whatever."

APPENDIX

APPENDIX.

An Act for the Commutation of Tithes in England and Wales, 13th August, 1836.

Whereas it is expedient to amend the laws relating to tithes in England and Wales, and to provide the means for an adequate compensation for tithes, and for the commutation thereof: Be it therefore enacted by the King's most excellent Majesty, by and with the advice and consent of the Lords spiritual and temporal, and Commons, in this present parliament assembled, and by the authority of the same, that it shall be lawful for one of his majesty's principal secretaries of state to appoint two fit persons to be commissioners to carry this Act into execution, and for the Archbishop of Canterbury, under his hand and archiepiscopal seal, to appoint one fit person to be a commissioner to carry this Act into execution, and for the said archbishop and secretary of state, at their joint pleasure, to remove any one or more of the commissioners so appointed; and upon every vacancy in the office of commissioner some other fit person shall be appointed to the said office in the same manner and by the same authority as the commissioner whose vacancy is thereby supplied; and until such appointment it shall be lawful for the continuing commissioners or commissioner to act as if no such vacancy had occurred. *Appointment of commissioners.*

II. And be it enacted, that the said commissioners shall be styled "The Tithe Commissioners for England and Wales," and shall have their office in London or West- *Style of commissioners.*

minster, and they, or any two of them, may sit from time to time, as they deem expedient, as a board of commissioners for carrying this Act into execution; and the said commissioners shall cause to be made a seal of the said board, and shall cause to be sealed or stamped therewith all agreements and awards confirmed by the said commissioners in pursuance of this Act; and all such agreements and awards and other instruments proceeding from the said board, or copies thereof, purporting to be sealed or stamped with the seal of the said board, shall be received in evidence without any further proof thereof; and no agreement or award shall be of any force unless the same shall be sealed or stamped as aforesaid.

<small>*To have a common seal.*</small>

<small>*Awards, &c. purporting to be sealed with such seal to be received as evidence.*</small>

III. And be it enacted, that the said commissioners shall from time to time give to any one of his Majesty's principal secretaries of state such information respecting their proceedings, or any part thereof, as the said principal secretary of state shall require, and shall once in every year send to one of the principal secretaries of state a general report of their proceedings; and every year such general report shall be laid before both Houses of Parliament within six weeks after the receipt of the same by such principal secretary of state if parliament be sitting, or if parliament be not sitting, then within six weeks after the next meeting thereof.

<small>*Commissioners to report to secretary of state.*</small>

<small>*Annual report to be laid before parliament.*</small>

IV. And be it enacted, that it shall be lawful for the commissioners from time to time to appoint a sufficient number of persons to be assistant commissioners, and also a secretary and assistant secretary, and all such clerks, messengers, and officers as they shall deem necessary, and to remove such assistant commissioners, secretary or assistant secretary, clerks, messengers, or officers, or any of them, and on any vacancy in any of the said offices to appoint some other person to the vacant office; and the persons so appointed shall assist in carrying this Act into execution at such places and in such manner as the said commissioners may direct: provided always that the said commissioners shall not appoint more than twelve such assistant commissioners to act at any one time, unless the lord high treasurer, or any three or more of the commissioners of his Majesty's treasury, shall, in the case of each such appointment, consent

<small>*Power to appoint assistant commissioners, secretary, assistant secretary, &c.*</small>

<small>*Limiting the number of appointments.*</small>

thereto; provided further, that the number of such clerks, messengers, and officers, shall be subject to the like consent.

V. And be it enacted, that no commissioner or assistant commissioner appointed as aforesaid shall during his continuance in such office be capable of being elected or of sitting as a member of the House of Commons. *Commissioners not to sit in the House of Commons.*

VI. And be it enacted, that no commissioner or assistant commissioner, secretary, assistant secretary, or other officer or person so to be appointed, shall hold his office for a longer period than five years next after the day of the passing of this Act, and thenceforth until the end of the then next session of parliament; and after the expiration of the said period of five years and of the then next session of parliament so much of this Act as authorises any such appointment shall cease. *Operation of Act as to appointment of commissioners, &c. limited to five years.*

VII. And be it enacted, that the salaries of the commissioners, the allowance to the assistant commissioners, and the salaries of the secretary, assistant secretary, clerks, messengers, and other officers to be appointed under this Act, shall be from time to time regulated by the lord treasurer or the lords commissioners of his Majesty's treasury, or any three of them: provided always that the salary of a commissioner shall not exceed the sum of one thousand five hundred pounds a year, nor the allowance to an assistant commissioner the sum of three pounds for every day that he shall be actually employed or travelling in the performance of the duties of his office, nor the salaries of the secretary or assistant secretary the sum of eight hundred pounds a year; and that the salaries of the clerks, messengers, and other officers shall be in fit proportion: provided also, that the said lord treasurer or lords commissioners may allow to any commissioner, assistant commissioner, secretary, assistant secretary, clerk, messenger, or other officer, any such reasonable travelling and other expenses as may have been incurred by him in the performance of his duties under this Act, in addition to his salary or allowance respectively. *Salaries of and allowances to commissioners and assistant commissioners, secretary, and other officers.*

VIII. And be it enacted, that the salaries, allowances, and travelling and other expenses of the commissioners, assistant commissioners, secretary, assistant secretary, clerks, messengers, and officers as aforesaid, and all other incidental *Such salaries, allowances, and other expenses, how to be paid.*

expenses of carrying this Act into execution, not herein otherwise provided for, shall be paid by the lord treasurer or the lords commissioners of his Majesty's treasury out of the consolidated fund.

<small>Commissioners and assistant commissioners to take an oath.</small>

IX. And be it enacted, that every such commissioner and assistant commissioner shall, before he shall enter upon the execution of his office, take the following oath before one of the judges of his Majesty's Court of King's Bench or Common Pleas, or one of the barons of the Court of Exchequer (that is to say):

<small>Form of oath.</small>

"I *A.B.* do swear that I will faithfully, impartially, and honestly, according to the best of my skill and judgment, fulfil all the powers and duties of a commissioner [*or* assistant commissioner, *as the case may be*] under an Act passed in the   year of the reign of King William the Fourth, intituled [*here set forth the title of this Act*]."

<small>Notification of appointment to be published in the Gazette.</small>

And the appointment of every such commissioner and assistant commissioner, with the time when and the name of the judge or baron before whom he shall have taken the oath aforesaid, shall be forthwith published in the "London Gazette."

<small>Commissioners or assistant commissioner may summon and examine witnesses.</small>

X. And be it enacted, that the said commissioners, or any assistant commissioner, may, by summons under their or his hand, require the attendance of all such persons as they or he may think fit to examine upon any matter brought before them or him as hereinafter mentioned relating to the commutation of tithes, and also make any inquiries and call for any answer or return as to any such matter, and also administer oaths, and examine all such persons upon oath, and cause to be produced before them or him upon oath all books, deeds, contracts, agreements, accounts, and writings, terriers, maps, plans, and surveys, or copies thereof respectively, in anywise relating to any such matter: provided always that no such person shall be required, in obedience to any such summons, to travel more than ten miles from the place of his abode, or to produce any deeds, papers, or writings relating to the title of any lands or tithes.

<small>Commissioners may delegate</small>

XI. And be it enacted, that the said commissioners may delegate to their assistant commissioners, or to any one or more of them, such of the powers hereby given to the said commissioners as the said commissioners shall think fit (except the power to confirm agreements and awards, or to frame forms of agreements and other instruments, as hereinafter provided, or to do any act herein required to be done under the seal of the said commissioners), and the powers so delegated shall be exercised under such regulations as the said commissioners shall direct; and the said commissioners may at any time recall or alter all or any of the powers delegated as aforesaid, and, notwithstanding the delegation thereof, may act as if no such delegation had been made; and all acts done by any such assistant commissioner in pursuance of such delegated powers shall be obeyed by all persons as if they had proceeded from the said commissioners, and the non-observance thereof shall be punishable in like manner. *[powers to assistant commissioners, except the powers to be exercised under their seal.]*

XII. And be it enacted, that in the construction and for the purposes of this Act, unless there be something in the subject or context repugnant to such construction, the word "person" shall mean and include the King's Majesty, and anybody corporate, aggregate, or sole, as well as an individual; and any word importing the singular number only shall mean and include several persons or parties as well as one person or party, and several things as well as one thing respectively, and the converse; and any word importing the masculine gender only shall mean and include a female as well as a male; and the word "lands" shall mean and include all messuages, lands, tenements, and hereditaments; and the word "tithes" shall mean and include all uncommuted tithes, portions and parcels of tithes, and all moduses, compositions real, and prescriptive and customary payments; and the word "parish" and "parochial" shall mean and include and extend to every parish and every extra-parochial place, and every township or village, within which overseers of the poor are separately appointed under the provisions of an act passed in the thirteenth and fourteenth years of the reign of his late Majesty King Charles the Second, intituled "An Act for the better Relief of the Poor of this Kingdom," and every district of which the tithes are payable under a separate impropriation or appropriation, or in a separate portion or parcel, or which the commissioners shall by any *[Meaning of the words "person," "lands," "tithes," "parish," "parochial," "land owner," "tithe owner," as used in this Act.]* *[13 & 14 Car. 2. c. 12.]*

order direct to be considered as a separate district for the commutation of tithes; and the words "land owner" or "tithe owner," or "owner of lands" or "owner of tithes," shall mean and include every person who shall be in the actual possession or receipt of the rents or profits of any lands or tithes (except any tenant for life or lives, or for years, holding under a lease or agreement for a lease on which a rent of not less than two thirds of the clear yearly value of the premises comprised therein shall have been reserved, and except any tenant for years whatsoever under a lease or agreement for a lease for a term which shall not have exceeded fourteen years from the commencement thereof), and that without regard to the real amount of interest of such person; and in every case in which any tithes or lands shall have been leased or agreed to be leased to any person for life or lives, or for years, by any lease or agreement for a lease on which a rent less than two-thirds of the clear yearly value of the premises comprised therein shall have been reserved, and of which the term shall have exceeded fourteen years from the commencement thereof, the person who shall for the time being be in the actual receipt of the rent reserved upon such lease or agreement for a lease shall, jointly with the person who shall be liable to the payment of such rent of such tithes or lands, be deemed for the purposes of this Act to be the owner of such tithes or lands; and in every case in which any person shall be in possession or receipt of the rents or profits of any tithes or lands under any sequestration, extent, elegit, or other writ of execution, or as a receiver under any order of a court of equity, the person against whom such writ shall have issued, or who but for such order would have been in possession, shall, jointly with the person in possession by virtue of such writ or order, be deemed for the purposes of this Act to be the owner of such tithes or lands.

Where parties to be deemed joint owners.

When the ownership of lands or tithes or patronage is vested in the Crown, who shall be deemed the

XIII. And be it enacted, that whenever the ownership of any lands or tithes to which the provisions of this Act are intended to apply shall be vested in his Majesty, the first commissioner of his Majesty's woods, forests, and land revenues for the time being, or in case such lands or tithes shall be vested in his Majesty in right of the Duchy of Lancaster or of the Duchy of Cornwall, the chancellor of the Duchy of Lancaster, or the officers of the Duchy of Cornwall, entitled to grant leases of lands parcel of the Duchy of Cornwall, shall for the purposes of this Act be substituted instead of the owner of such lands or tithes respectively; and whenever the patronage of any benefice to which the provisions of this Act are intended to apply shall be vested in his Majesty, the lord high treasurer or first lord commissioner of the treasury for the time being where the value of such benefice is above the yearly value of twenty pounds in the King's books, and where such value is of or below the yearly value of twenty pounds in the King's books, the lord chancellor, or lord keeper, or first lord commissioner of the great seal for the time being, shall for the purposes of this Act be substituted instead of the patron: provided, nevertheless, that if such patronage is vested in his Majesty in right of the Duchy of Lancaster, the chancellor for the time being of such duchy shall for the purposes of this Act be substituted instead of the patron. *owner or patron.*

XIV. And be it enacted, that whenever any person shall be at the same time owner of any lands and owner of any tithes comprised within any agreement to be executed pursuant to the provisions of this Act, or besides being owner of any lands or of any tithes shall also be patron of the benefice to which the tithes in question may belong, such person, in relation to such agreement, may act and be dealt with in each of the several characters so borne by him as aforesaid. *When the same person is owner of lands and owner of tithes, he may be dealt with in both characters.*

XV. And be it enacted, that whenever the patron of any benefice or the owner of any lands or tithes to which the provisions of this Act are intended to apply, or any person interested in any question as to any tithes, shall be a minor, idiot, lunatic, feme covert, beyond the seas, or under any other legal disability, the guardian, trustee, committee of the estate, husband, or attorney respectively, or in default thereof such person as may be nominated for that purpose by the commissioners after due inquiry shall have been made by them as to the fitness of such person, and whom they are hereby empowered to nominate under their hands and seal, shall for the purposes of this Act be substituted in the place of such patron, owner, or person so interested. *In case the patron or owner is under legal disability, who to act.*

XVI. And be it enacted, that it shall be lawful for any land owner or tithe owner, by a power of attorney given in writing under his hand, to appoint an agent to act for him in carrying into execution the provisions of this Act; and all things which by this Act are directed to be done by or with relation to any person may be lawfully done by or with relation to the agent so duly authorised of such person; and every such agent shall have full power, in the name and on behalf of his principal, to concur in and execute any agreement, and to vote on any question arising out of the execution of this Act; and every person shall be bound by the acts of any such agent, according to the authority committed to him, as fully as if the principal of such agent had so acted; and the power of attorney under which the agent shall have acted, or a copy thereof authenticated by the signature of two credible witnesses, shall be appended to every agreement executed by any such agent, and shall be sent with it to the office of the commissioners as hereinafter provided; and any such power of attorney may be in the form following:

Acts may be done by agents duly authorised.

" I *A. B.* of [*&c.*] do hereby appoint *C. D.* of [*&c.*] to be my lawful attorney, to act for me in all respects as if I myself were present and acting in the execution of an Act passed in the sixth and seventh years of his present Majesty, intituled [*here insert the title of this Act*].

Power of attorney.

(Signed) " *A. B.*"

XVII. And be it enacted, that any one or more of the land owners or tithe owners, whose interest respectively shall not be less than one fourth part of the whole value of the lands subject to tithes, or one fourth part of the whole value of the tithes of any parish in England or Wales, may call a parochial meeting of land owners and tithe owners within the limits of the parish, by notice thereof in writing under his or their hand, to be affixed at least twenty-one days before such meeting on the principal outer door of the church, or in some public and conspicuous place within the limits of the parish, and to be twice at least during such twenty-one days inserted in some newspaper generally circulated within the county in which such parish is situated, for the purpose of making an agreement for the general

Parochial meetings may be called, at which owners of two-thirds in value may agree on the sum to be paid to the tithe owners, which agreement shall bind the whole parish.

commutation of tithes within the limits of such parish; and every land owner and tithe owner attending such meeting shall bear his own expenses of attendance; and the land owners and tithe owners who shall be present at any such meeting called as aforesaid, and whose interest in the lands and tithes of the parish respectively shall not be less than two-thirds of the lands subject to tithes, two-thirds of the great tithes and two-thirds of the small tithes of the parish, may proceed to make and execute a parochial agreement for the payment of an annual sum by way of rent-charge, variable as hereinafter provided, instead of the great and small tithes of the parish collectively, or instead of the great tithes and small tithes severally, to the respective owners thereof in the said parish; and every agreement so made and executed, and confirmed in manner hereinafter mentioned, shall be binding on all persons interested in the tithes or lands subject to tithes of the said parish.

XVIII. And be it enacted, that the majority of such land owners and tithe owners present at every such meeting shall elect a chairman, who shall forthwith proceed to ascertain the interest of the land owners and tithe owners then present in person or by their agents; and in case it shall thereupon appear that the persons present at such meeting have not a sufficient interest in the premises as aforesaid to make and execute such an agreement which shall be binding on all persons interested therein, it shall be lawful, notwithstanding, for any number of the persons then present to make and execute a provisional agreement for the commutation of tithes of the like form and tenor; and every such provisional agreement which shall be executed within six calendar months from the day of the first making thereof by the land owners and tithe owners whose interest in the lands and tithes of the parish shall not be less than two-thirds of the lands subject to tithes, two-thirds of the great tithes, and two-thirds of the small tithes of the parish respectively, shall be as binding as if executed by all the parties thereto at the meeting at which the agreement was first made. *Provisional agreements may be made at the parochial meetings.*

XIX. Provided always, and be it enacted, that the proportional interest of the owners of such lands or tithes, so far as relates to their power to make any such agreement or *Proportional interest in lands and tithes how* provisional agreement, or to give any notice to the commissioners or assistant-commissioners as herein-after provided, shall be estimated according to the proportional sum at which such lands or tithes shall be rated to the relief of the poor, or if there shall be no such rate, according to the rules by which property of the same kind is by law rateable to the relief of the poor.

<small>*to be estimated for the purposes of this Act.*</small>

XX. And be it enacted, that in case an adjournment of the said meeting for any cause shall be desired by a majority of the persons attending such meeting, the chairman shall adjourn the meeting to any time and place then by him to be declared, and so from time to time in case the same shall be in like manner desired by a majority of the persons attending such meeting; and notice of every adjourned meeting shall be given under the hand of the chairman, and shall be affixed in a conspicuous place on the outside of the building in which such meeting, or the last adjournment thereof, shall have been holden; and the like order of proceeding shall be observed at any such adjourned meeting, and everything done at any such adjourned meeting shall be as valid as if done at the original meeting.

<small>*Meeting may be adjourned.*</small>

XXI. And be it enacted, that every such agreement shall bear date on the day on which the first signature is attached thereto, and every such agreement or some schedule thereunto annexed shall set forth all the lands of the said parish which are subject to the payment of any kind of tithes, and also the true or estimated quantity in statute measure or land subject to tithes within the parish which shall be then cultivated as arable, meadow, or pasture land, or as wood land, common land, or howsoever otherwise, and shall also set forth whether any modus or composition real, or prescriptive or customary payment, shall be payable instead of all or any of the tithes of the said parish, and which lands or tithes respectively are covered thereby, and shall also set forth which of the said tithes, moduses, compositions, or payments are payable to the tithe owner, or if there is more than one tithe owner to each of the several tithe owners in the said parish, distinguishing in what right every such tithe owner is entitled to such tithes, and shall also set forth whether any and which of the lands of the said parish are or have

<small>*Form of parochial agreement.*</small>

been under any and what circumstances exempt from the payment of any and what tithes; and such agreement shall also state in words at length the amount of the sum or sums agreed to be paid (subject to variation as hereinafter provided) instead of the tithes of the lands comprised in the said agreement, and instead of all moduses and compositions real, prescriptive and customary payments (if any), payable in respect of such lands, or the produce of such lands or any of them, distinguishing, if there is more than one tithe owner, the sum payable to every such tithe owner, and where the tithes of different lands in the same parish are payable to different tithe owners, or to the same tithe owner in different rights, distinguishing the sum payable in respect of such different lands; and every such agreement shall also state all such other particulars as the commissioners shall by any order from time to time require to be inserted in such agreements.

XXII. And be it enacted, that the commissioners shall frame and cause to be printed, as soon as conveniently may be after their appointment, forms of notices and agreements, and such other instruments as in their judgment will further the purposes of this Act, and supply all or any of such forms to the churchwardens and overseers of any parish who may require the same, or to whom the commissioners may think fit to send the same for the use of any land owner or tithe owner desirous of putting this act in execution. *Commissioners to frame and circulate forms of agreements, &c.*

XXIII. And be it enacted, that any commissioner or assistant commissioner, if the commissioners shall think fit, may attend any such meeting for the purpose of taking part in the discussion and advising on the terms of agreement; but no commissioner or assistant commissioner, during the time that he is is actually attending such meeting for that purpose, shall have any of the powers herein given to the commissioners in case of an award or apportionment by the commissioners as hereinafter provided. *Commissioner or assistant commissioner may attend to advise terms of agreement.*

XXIV. And be it enacted, that if any suit shall be pending touching the right to any tithes, or if there shall be any question as to the existence of any modus or composition real, or prescriptive or customary payment, or any claim of exemption from or non-liability to tithes, under any circum- *Suits and differences may be referred to arbitration.*

stances, in respect of any lands or any kind of produce, or touching the situation or boundary of any lands, or if any difference shall arise whereby the making and executing of any such agreement shall be hindered, it shall be lawful for the owners, or, if there shall be no owner actually in possession, for the persons claiming to be the owners, of the lands and tithes respectively, being parties to such suit or difference, to submit the same to reference by any writing under their respective hands, containing an agreement that such submission shall be made a rule of any of his Majesty's Courts of Record, upon such terms of reference as the parties may agree upon; and the decision of the arbitrator or arbitrators named in the said reference shall for the purposes of this Act be final and conclusive on all persons: provided, nevertheless, that no person being owner of an estate in land or tithes, less in the whole than an immediate estate of fee simple or fee tail, shall be empowered to submit to any such reference so as to bind any person in remainder, reversion, or expectancy, without the consent of the commissioners; and that it shall be lawful for the commissioners, if they shall think fit so to do, but not otherwise necessary, to direct that any person in remainder, reversion, or expectancy of an estate of inheritance in the said lands or tithes, or any other person whom they shall deem to be interested therein, shall be made a party to such reference.

Agreements pending at the time of the passing of this Act, if completed and confirmed by the commissioners, to be as valid as parochial agreements.

XXV. And be it enacted, that every agreement for the commutation for a rent-charge of the tithes of any lands which shall be pending at the time of the passing of this Act, and which shall be executed before or within six calendar months after the passing of this Act by the land owners and tithe owners, or persons claiming to be such owners, whose interest in the said lands and tithes shall not be less than two thirds of the said lands, two-thirds of the great tithes and two-thirds of the small tithes of the said lands, and which shall be confirmed by the commissioners, under their hands and seal, in the manner hereinafter provided for the confirmation of any parochial agreement, shall be as valid, and the rent-charge agreed to be paid by any such agreement shall be apportioned and charged, as hereinafter provided, among and upon the said lands, as if the agreement had been made and executed at a parochial meeting.

XXVI. Provided always, and be it enacted, that in every case in which any tithes shall belong to any ecclesiastical person in right of any spiritual dignity or benefice, no agreement for the commutation of such tithes made and executed under this Act shall be deemed to be executed by the owner of such tithes unless such consent thereto be given as is hereinafter mentioned; (that is to say,) in the case of an archbishop or bishop, the consent of the crown signified by the lord high treasurer or first lord commissioner of the treasury; and in case of the incumbent of any other benefice or ecclesiastical dignity, the consent of the patron or person entitled to present to such benefice or dignity in case the same were then vacant; and every such consent shall be given under the hand of the person giving the same, and shall be annexed to the agreement, and taken to be part of the execution thereof.

Consent of patron to be given to every agreement for commutation of ecclesiastical tithe.

XXVII. And be it enacted, that every such agreement, as soon as may be after it shall have been executed by a sufficient number of land owners and tithe owners whose interest in the lands and tithes of the parish respectively shall not be less than two thirds of the lands subject to tithes, two thirds of the great tithes and two thirds of the small tithes, shall be sent by the chairman of the meeting, or by the person in whose custody it shall then be, to the office of the commissioners, and the commissioners, by themselves, or by some assistant commissioner, shall cause inquiry to be made and shall require such proof as will be satisfactory to them, whether or not the agreement has been made without fraud or collusion, and whether or not it ought to be confirmed; and if they shall be satisfied that it ought to be confirmed, the commissioners shall confirm the agreement under their hands and seal, and shall add to such agreement the date of the confirmation, and shall publish the fact of such confirmation and the date thereof within the parish in such manner as to them shall seem fit; and every such confirmed agreement shall be binding on all persons interested in the said lands or tithes.

Agreement to be confirmed by the commissioners.

XXVIII. Provided always, and be it enacted, that before the commissioners shall confirm any such agreement relating to tithes belonging to any ecclesiastical person in right of

Agreement to be communicated to bishop of

APPENDIX.

<small>the diocese previous to its being confirmed.</small>

any spiritual dignity or benefice, they shall communicate the same to the bishop of the diocese for his observations and opinion; and no such agreement shall be confirmed by such commissioners until four weeks shall have elapsed from the date of the transmission of such agreement to such bishop, unless the said bishop shall sooner signify his approbation of such agreement to the said commissioners.

<small>Land, not exceeding twenty acres, may be given as commutation for tithes, &c.</small>

XXIX. And be it enacted, that any such parochial agreement may be made in manner and form aforesaid for giving to any ecclesiastical owner, in right of any spiritual benefice or dignity, of any tithes or of any rent-charge for which such tithes shall have been commuted, any quantity not exceeding in the whole twenty imperial acres of land by way of commutation for the whole or an equivalent part of the great or small tithes of the parish, or in discharge of or exchange for the whole or an equivalent part of any rent-charge agreed to be paid instead of such tithes, but subject in every case to the provisions hereinafter contained; and every such agreement shall be made in such form and contain such particulars as the commissioners shall in that behalf direct, specifying the land whereof the tithes or rent-charge for which such tithes shall have been commuted shall be the subject of such agreement, and giving full and sufficient descriptions of the quantity, state of culture, and annual value of the land proposed to be given in exchange for such tithes or rent-charge: provided always, that the same consent and confirmation shall be necessary to any such agreement as in the case of an agreement for a rent-charge; and that in case the said agreement shall not extend to the whole of the tithes of the parish, an agreement or award as hereinafter provided may and shall be made for the payment of a rent-charge in satisfaction of the residue of the said tithes; and such rent-charge when agreed upon or awarded, or the residue thereof, shall be apportioned in manner hereinafter provided upon all the lands of the parish subject to the payment of tithes, unless otherwise agreed upon by the parties to the said parochial agreement, except the land so given by way of commutation, in like manner as if no agreement for giving land had been made: provided also, that the land so given shall be free from incumbrances, except leases at improved rent, land tax, or other usual outgoings, and shall not be of leasehold tenure, nor of copyhold or customary tenure, subject to arbitrary fine or the render of heriots.

XXX. And be it enacted, that in every case in which any such agreement for giving land shall be so entered into, the commissioners shall satisfy themselves, in such way and by such evidence as they shall see fit, of the title to the land proposed thereby to be given in exchange for such tithes or rent-charge, and that the same are of the description and value set forth in such agreement, and that such agreement is conformable in every respect to the provisions hereinbefore contained respecting the same; and the expense attending every such agreement for giving land, and the confirmation thereof, and of investigating the title of the land, shall be borne by the owners of land liable to the payment of tithes within the parish, in such proportions as they may agree, or, in default of agreement, as the commissioners may direct. *Commissioners to satisfy themselves of the title of such land, &c.*

XXXI. And be it enacted, that such agreement for giving land, confirmed by the said commissioners, shall operate as a conveyance of such land to the owner of such tithes or rent-charge, and the land so conveyed shall thereupon vest in and be and be deemed to be holden by such person or persons, and upon the like uses and trusts in every respect as the tithes or rent-charge in commutation or exchange for which the same shall have been given shall be vested and holden; and for the purpose of making and completing any such agreement the provisions of this Act respecting persons under legal disability shall apply to every person party to such agreement or in whom any such land shall be vested, and whose concurrence or consent may be necessary to the perfecting thereof, or of the title to such land, as fully as if the same had been here repeated and re-enacted. *Agreements for giving land to operate as conveyances.*

XXXII. And be it enacted, that at the said meeting or at some adjournment thereof, or at some other parochial meeting to be called in like manner, either before or after the confirmation of the agreement, the owners of lands subject to tithes in the said parish, or their agents, present at the meeting, may appoint a valuer or valuers; and in case *Appointment of valuers.*

the majority in respect of number and the majority in respect of interest shall not agree upon the appointment, then they shall appoint two or such other even number of valuers as shall be then agreed on by such land owners, half of such number to be chosen by a majority in respect of number, and the other half by a majority in respect of interest, of such land owners then present.

Valuers to apportion the rent-charge.

XXXIII. And be it enacted, that as soon as may be after the choosing of such valuer or valuers, and after the confirmation of the said agreement, the valuer or valuers so chosen shall apportion the total sum agreed to be paid by way of rent-charge instead of tithes, and the expenses of the apportionment, amongst the several lands in the said parish, according to such principles of apportionment as shall be agreed upon at the meeting at which the valuer or valuers shall be chosen, or if no principles shall be then agreed upon for the guidance of the valuer or valuers, then, having regard to the average titheable produce and productive quality of the lands, according to his or their discretion and judgment, but subject in each case to the provisions hereinafter contained, and so that in each case the several lands shall have the full benefit of every modus and composition real, prescriptive and customary payment, and of every exemption from or non-liability to tithes relating to the said lands respectively, and having regard to the several tithes to which the said lands are severally liable; provided that it shall be lawful for the said valuers, when an even number is chosen, by any writing under their hands, to appoint an umpire before they proceed upon the business of such apportionment, and the decision of the umpire on the questions in difference between the valuers shall be binding on them, and shall be adopted by them in the apportionment.

Valuers may enter on lands for the purpose of valuing tithes.

XXXIV. And be it enacted, that the said valuers and umpire (if it shall become necessary for him to act), and their agents or servants, at all reasonable times, may enter upon any of the lands to be included in the apportionment, and make an admeasurement, plan, and valuation of the same, without being subject to any action or molestation for so doing: provided always, that no valuer or umpire shall be capable of acting until he shall have made and subscribed before the said commissioners, or some assistant commissioner or justice of the peace, a solemn declaration to the same purport and effect as the oath hereinbefore directed to be made by the said commissioners, substituting only the proper description of such person instead of the word commissioner, and adding to his signature the usual place of his residence, which declaration it shall be lawful for the said commissioners, or any assistant commissioner or justice, to administer; and every such declaration so made and subscribed shall be countersigned by the person before whom the same shall have been made, and shall be sent by him to the office of the commissioners.

XXXV. And be it enacted, that the valuer or valuers or umpire may, if they think fit, use for the purposes of this Act any admeasurement, plan, or valuation previously made of the lands or tithes in question of the accuracy of which they shall be satisfied; and that it shall be lawful for the meeting at which such valuer or valuers shall be chosen to agree upon the adoption for the purposes aforesaid of any such admeasurement, plan, or valuation, and such agreement shall be binding upon the valuer or valuers; provided always, that three fourths of the land owners in number and value shall concur therein. *Old plans and surveys may be used if the valuers think proper.*

XXXVI. And be it enacted, that after the first day of October, one thousand eight hundred and thirty-eight, the commissioners shall proceed in manner hereinafter mentioned, at such time and in such order as to them shall seem fit, either by themselves or by some assistant commissioner, to ascertain and award the total sum to be paid by way of rent-charge instead of the tithes of every parish in England and Wales, in which no such agreement binding upon the whole parish as aforesaid shall have been made and confirmed as aforesaid: provided nevertheless, that if any proceeding shall be had towards making and executing any such agreement after the commissioners shall have given or caused to be given notice of their intention to act as aforesaid in such parish, the commissioners may refrain from acting upon such notice, if they shall think fit, until the result of such proceeding shall appear. *After 1st Oct. 1838, commissioners may ascertain total value of tithes in any parish in which no previous agreement has been made.*

138   APPENDIX.

Value of tithes to be calculated upon an average of seven years.

XXXVII. And be it enacted, that in every case in which the commissioners shall intend making such award, notice thereof shall be given in such manner as to them shall seem fit; and after the expiration of twenty-one days after such notice shall have been given, the commissioners or some assistant commissioner shall, except in the cases for which provision is hereinafter made, proceed to ascertain the clear average value (after making all just deductions on account of the expenses of collecting, preparing for sale, and marketing where such tithes have been taken in kind) of the tithes of the said parish, according to the average of seven years preceding Christmas in the year one thousand eight hundred and thirty-five: provided that if during the said period of seven years, or any part thereof, the said tithes or any part thereof shall have been compounded for or demised to the owner or occupier of any of the said lands in consideration of any rent or payment instead of tithes, the amount of such composition or rent or sum agreed to be paid instead of tithes shall be taken as the clear value of the tithes included in such composition, demise, or agreement during the time for which the same shall have been made; and the commissioners or assistant commissioner shall award the average annual value of the said seven years so ascertained as the sum to be taken for calculating the rent-charge to be paid as a permanent commutation of the said tithes: provided also, that whenever it shall appear to the commissioners that the party entitled to any such rent or composition shall in any one or more of the said seven years have allowed and made any abatement from the amount of such rent or composition on the ground of the same having in any such year or years been higher than the sum fairly payable by way of composition for the tithe, but not otherwise, then and in every such case such diminished amount, after making such abatement as aforesaid, shall be deemed and taken to have been the sum agreed to be paid for any such year or years:

Tithes to be valued without deduction on account of parochial and county rates, &c.

provided also, that in estimating the value of the said tithes the commissioners or assistant commissioner shall estimate the same without making any deduction therefrom on account of any parliamentary, parochial, county and other rates, charges, and assessments to which the said tithes are liable; and whenever the said tithes shall have been demised or compounded for on the principle of the rent or composition being paid free from all such rates, charges, and assessments, or any part thereof, the said commissioners or assistant commissioner shall have regard to that circumstance, and shall make such an addition on account thereof as shall be an equivalent.

XXXVIII. Provided always, and be it enacted, that in case notice in writing under the hand of any patron, or the hands of any land owners or tithe owners whose interest in the lands or tithes of the parish shall not be less than one half of the lands subject to tithes, one half of the great tithes or one half of the small tithes of the parish, shall be given to the commissioners or assistant commissioner acting in that behalf, within one calendar month next after the notice of the intention to make an award shall have been given as aforesaid, that the average value to be ascertained as aforesaid will not fairly represent the sum which ought to be taken for calculating a permanent commutation of the great or small tithes of the said parish, the commissioners shall have power to diminish or increase the sum to be so taken by a sum amounting to not more than one fifth part of the average value ascertained as aforesaid: provided always, that every case which shall appear to the commissioners to be fraudulent or collusive, or which, by reason of the length of time which shall have elapsed since the making of any composition then in force, or which, by reason of the peculiar interest in the lands or tithes of either of the parties to any composition, or by reason of any other special circumstances, ought in the judgment of the commissioners to be separately adjudicated upon, shall be reserved for separate adjudication as hereinafter provided; and the commissioners shall certify and report to one of his Majesty's principal secretaries of state, under their hands and seals, before the first day of May in the year one thousand eight hundred and thirty-eight, in what manner the discretion hereby vested in them ought in their judgment to be exercised, and shall in the said report lay down such rules for the guidance of the assistant commissioners as may to them seem expedient; and such report shall be laid before parliament within six weeks after the same shall have been received or after the meeting of

Commissioners in certain cases may increase or diminish the sum to be paid for commutation.

parliament, and, unless parliament shall otherwise provide, such rules shall be observed by the said commissioners and assistant commissioners in the exercise of the discretion hereby vested in the commissioners.

Special adjudications how to be made.

XXXIX. And be it enacted, that the commissioners shall from time to time report to one of his Majesty's principal secretaries of state, under their hands and seals, all the cases which under the power hereinbefore reserved to them in that behalf shall have been reserved for separate adjudication, and shall state in every such report the reasons for so reserving every case mentioned therein, and the commissioners shall in every such case award the rent-charge to be paid as a permanent commutation for tithes, having regard to the average rate which shall be awarded in respect of lands of the like description and similarly situated in the neighbouring parishes; provided always, that a draft of such intended award, with a copy of so much of the said report as is applicable to such award, shall be deposited in the parish; and the commissioners, or an assistant commissioner to be specially appointed by the commissioners for that purpose, shall hear and determine all objections to the award in the like manner as is herein provided in an ordinary case of award, and the commissioners shall have power thereupon to amend the draft of the said award accordingly.

How the tithe of hops, fruit, and garden produce is to be valued.

XL. And be it enacted, that in case any of the lands in the parish shall be hop grounds, orchards, or gardens, and notice shall be given by the owner thereof to the commissioners or assistant commissioner acting in that behalf, that the tithes thereof should be separately valued, the commissioners or assistant commissioner shall estimate the value of the tithes thereof according to the average rate of composition for the tithes of hops, fruit, and garden produce respectively during seven years preceding Christmas in the year one thousand eight hundred and thirty-five, within a district to be assigned in each case by the commissioners or assistant commissioner, and estimating the same as chargeable to all parliamentary, parochial, county, and other rates, charges, and assessments to which the said tithes are liable, and shall add the value so estimated to the value of the other tithes of the parish ascertained as aforesaid.

APPENDIX. 141

XLI. And be it enacted, that in case any of the lands in the parish shall be coppices, and notice shall be given by the owner thereof, or by the owner of the tithes thereof, to the commissioners or assistant commissioner acting in that behalf, that the tithes thereof should be separately valued, the commissioners or assistant commissioner shall estimate the value of the tithes thereof with a due regard to the average value, estimated according to the best of their judgment, of coppice wood of the same kind cut during the said period of seven years in that parish and the neighbouring parishes, estimating the same as chargeable to all parliamentary, parochial, county, and other rates, charges, and assessments to which the said tithes are liable, and shall add the clear value of the tithes so estimated to the value of the other tithes of the parish ascertained as aforesaid; and the commissioners shall, in the report which they are hereinbefore required to make to one of his Majesty's principal secretaries of state before the first day of May in the year one thousand eight hundred and thirty-eight, lay down rules for the guidance of the assistant commissioners in estimating the value of the tithes of coppice wood, and, unless parliament shall otherwise provide, such rules shall be observed by the said commissioners and assistant commissioners.

How the tithe of coppice wood is to be valued.

XLII. And be it enacted, that the amount which shall be charged by any such apportionment as hereinafter provided upon any hop grounds or market gardens in any district so to be assigned shall be distinguished into two parts, which shall be called the ordinary charge and the extraordinary charge, and the extraordinary charge shall be a rate per imperial acre, and so in proportion for less quantities of ground, according to the discretion of the valuers or commissioners or assistant commissioner by whom the apportionment shall be made as aforesaid; and all lands whereof the tithes shall have been commuted under this Act, and which shall cease to be cultivated as hop grounds or market gardens at any time after such commutation, shall be charged after the thirty-first day of December next following such change of cultivation only with the ordinary charge upon such lands; and all lands in any such district the tithes whereof shall have been commuted under this Act,

Provision for the change of culture of hop grounds and market gardens.

and which shall be newly cultivated as hop grounds or market gardens at any time after such commutation, shall be charged with an additional amount of rent-charge per imperial acre, equal to the extraordinary charge per acre upon hop grounds or market gardens respectively in that district: provided always, that no such additional amount shall be charged or payable during the first year, and half only of such additional amount during the second year, of such new cultivation; and an additional rent-charge by way of extraordinary charge upon hop grounds and market gardens, newly cultivated as such beyond the limits of every district in which any extraordinary charge for hop grounds or market gardens respectively shall have been distinguished as aforesaid at the time of the commutation, shall be charged by the commissioners at the time of such new cultivation, upon the request of any person interested therein, if such new cultivation shall have taken place during the continuance of the commission of the said commissioners, and after the expiration of the commission shall be charged in such manner and by such authority as parliament shall direct, and shall be payable and recoverable in like manner and subject to the same incidents in all respects as an extraordinary charge charged upon any hop grounds or market gardens at the time of commutation.

Provision for valuing tithes of lands to which the average of seven years cannot apply.

XLIII. And be it enacted, that in case any of the lands in the parish shall, during any part of the said period of seven years preceding Christmas in the year one thousand eight hundred and thirty-five, have been exempted from payment of tithes by reason of having been enclosed under any act of parliament, or converted from barren heath or waste ground, or by reason of being glebe lands, or of having been heretofore parcel of the possessions of any privileged order, and notice shall have been given as last aforesaid to the commissioners or assistant commissioner acting in that behalf that the tithes thereof should be separately valued, the commissioners or assistant commissioner shall estimate the value of the tithes thereof according to the average value which shall be ascertained as aforesaid in respect of lands of the like description and quality in that parish and the neighbouring parishes, or as near thereto as the circumstances of each case may in their judgment require, and estimating the same as chargeable to all parliamentary, parochial, county, and other rates, charges, and assessments to which the said tithes are liable, and shall add the value so estimated to the value of the other tithes of the parish ascertained as aforesaid.

XLIV. And be it enacted, that if any modus or composition real, or prescriptive or customary payment, shall be payable instead of the tithes of any of the lands or produce thereof in the said parish, the commissioners or assistant commissioner shall in such case estimate the amount of such modus, composition, or payment as the value of the tithes payable in respect of such lands or produce respectively, and shall add the amount thereof to the value of the other tithes of the parish ascertained as aforesaid, and shall also make due allowance for all exemptions from or non-liability to tithes of any lands or any part of the produce of such lands: provided also, that if it shall appear to the said commissioners or assistant commissioner that any question concerning any modus or composition real, prescriptive or customary payment, or claim of exemption from or non-liability to the payment of tithes relating to the lands in question, shall have been decided by competent authority before the making of the said award, the commissioners or assistant commissioners shall act on the principle established by such decision, and shall make their award as if such decision had been made at the beginning of the said period of seven years. *Moduses, &c. how to be allowed for in the award.*

XLV. And be it enacted, that if any suit shall be pending touching the right to any tithes, or if there shall be any question as to the existence of any modus or composition real, or prescriptive or customary payment, or any claim of exemption from or non-liability under any circumstances to the payment of any tithes in respect of any lands or any kind of produce, or touching the situation or boundary of any lands, or if any difference shall arise whereby the making of any such award by the commissioners or assistant commissioner shall be hindered, it shall be lawful for the commissioners or assistant commissioner to appoint a time and place in or near the parish for hearing and determining the same; and the decision of the commissioners or assistant *Commissioners may hear and determine disputes;*

subject to appeal by an issue at law;

commissioner shall be final and conclusive on all persons, subject to the provisions hereinafter contained.

XLVI. Provided always, and be it enacted, that any person claiming to be interested in any lands or in the tithes thereof who shall be dissatisfied with any such decision of the commissioners or assistant commissioner may, if the yearly value of the payment to be made or withholden according to such decision shall exceed the sum of twenty pounds, cause an action to be brought in any of his Majesty's courts of law at Westminster against the person in whose favour such decision shall have been made, within three calendar months next after such decision shall have been notified in writing, in such manner as the commissioners or assistant commissioner shall direct, to the parties interested therein or to their known agents, in which action the plaintiff shall deliver a feigned issue, whereby such disputed right may be tried, and shall proceed to a trial at law of such issue at the sittings after the term or at the assizes then next or next but one after such action shall have been commenced to be holden for the county within which such lands or the greater part thereof are situated, with liberty nevertheless for the court in which the same shall have been commenced, or any judge of his Majesty's courts of law at Westminster, to extend the time for going to trial therein, or to direct the trial to be in another county if it shall seem fit to such court or judge so to do; and every defendant in any such action shall enter an appearance thereto, and accept such issue; but in case the parties shall differ as to the form of such issue, or in case the defendant shall fail to enter such appearance or accept such issue, then the same shall be settled under the direction of the court in which the action shall be brought, or by any judge of his Majesty's courts of law at Westminster, and the plaintiff may proceed thereon in like manner as if the defendant had appeared and accepted such issue; and the parties in such action shall produce to each other and their respective attornies or counsel, at such time and place as any judge may order before trial, and also to the court and jury upon the trial of any such issue, all books, deeds, papers, and writings, terriers, maps, plans, and surveys relating to the matters in issue in their respective custody or power; and it shall be lawful for the judge by whom any such action shall be tried, if he shall think fit, to direct the jury to find a verdict, subject to the opinion of the court upon a special case; and the verdict which shall be given in any such action, or the judgment of the court upon the case subject to which the same may be given, shall be final and binding upon all parties thereto, unless the court wherein such action shall be brought shall set aside such verdict and order a new trial to be had therein, which it shall be lawful for the said court to do, if it shall see fit: provided also, that in case any such decision shall involve a question of law only, and the parties in difference shall be agreed upon the facts relating thereto, and whereon such decision shall have been founded, the said commissioners or assistant commissioner, at the request of the person dissatisfied (such request to be made in writing within three calendar months after such decision, and at least fourteen days' previous notice in writing of such request to be given in like manner to the other parties in difference or to their known agents), shall direct a case to be stated for the opinion of such one of his Majesty's courts of law at Westminster as the commissioners or assistant commissioner shall think fit, which case shall be settled by them or him, or under their or his direction, in case the parties differ about the same, and may be set down for argument and be brought before the court in like manner as other cases are brought before the court; and the decision of such court upon every case so brought before it shall be binding upon all parties concerned therein: provided always, that after such verdict given and not set aside by the court, or after such decision of the court, the said commissioners or assistant commissioner shall be bound by such verdict or decision; and the cost of every such action, or of stating such case and obtaining a decision thereon, shall be in the discretion of the court in or by which the same shall be decided, which may order the same to be taxed by the proper officer of the court, and the like execution may be had for the same as if such costs had been recovered upon a judgment of record of the said court. *or by taking the opinion of a court of law thereon.*

XLVII. And be it enacted, that no proceeding of or before the commissioners or any assistant commissioner, or *Proceedings not to abate by death of parties.*

in any action, or in any case stated, or reference in pursuance of this Act, shall abate or cease by reason of the death of any person interested therein.

In case of deaths of parties before actions brought, &c. the same to be carried on and defended in their names.

XLVIII. And be it enacted, that if any person in whose favour any such decision of the commissioners or any assistant commissioner shall have been made shall die before any such action shall have been brought or case stated, and before the expiration of the time hereinbefore limited for that purpose, it shall be lawful for every person who might have brought such action, or have had such case stated, against the person so dying, to bring or have the same, within the time so limited as aforesaid, nominally against such person as if living, and to serve the said commissioners or assistant commissioner with process and notices relating thereto in the same manner as the person deceased might have been served therewith if living; and it shall be lawful for every person entitled to the benefit of such decision as aforesaid, or, in case of any such person being a minor, idiot, lunatic, feme covert, beyond the seas, or under any other legal disability, the guardian, trustee, committee of the estate, husband, or attorney respectively, or in default thereof such person as may be nominated for that purpose by the commissioners, and whom they are hereby empowered to nominate under their hands and seal, to appear and defend such action or argue such case; and proceedings shall be had therein in the same manner, and the rights of all persons shall be equally bound and concluded by the event of such action or the decision upon such case, as if such person had been living; and the costs of every such action or case shall be in the discretion of the court as aforesaid.

Statutes of limitation not to be affected.

XLIX. Provided always, and be it enacted, that nothing in this Act contained shall revive any right to tithes which now is or hereafter shall be barred by any law in force for shortening the time required in claims of modus decimandi or exemption from or discharge from tithes, or for the limitation of actions and suits relating to real property.

Commissioners to award total sum to be paid for the

L. And be it enacted, that as soon as all such suits and differences shall have been decided, or if there shall have been no suits or differences then as soon as the commissioners or assistant commissioner shall have ascertained and estimated as aforesaid the total value of all the tithes of the said parish, *tithes of the parish.* the commissioners or assistant commissioner shall frame the draft of an award, declaring that the sum ascertained as aforesaid shall be the amount of the rent-charge to be paid in respect of the tithes of the said parish, and every such draft shall contain all the particulars hereinbefore required to be inserted in any parochial agreement or any schedule thereto; provided always, that no such award shall be made for giving land instead of the tithes of the parish.

LI. And be it enacted, that as soon as the said draft shall have been made by the commissioners or assistant commissioner, they or he shall deposit a copy of the same and of any special report thereunto annexed at some convenient place within the said parish for the inspection of all persons interested in the said lands or tithes, and shall forthwith give notice in such manner as to the commissioners shall seem fit where the said copy may be inspected, and shall also in such notice appoint some convenient place and time (the first not earlier than twenty-one days from the first giving of such notice) for holding a meeting to hear objections to such intended award by any person interested therein; and the said commissioners or assistant commissioner at such meeting as aforesaid shall hear and determine any objections which may be then and there made to the said intended award, or adjourn the further hearing thereof, if they or he shall think proper, to a future meeting, and may, if they or he shall see occasion, direct any further valuation of the lands or tithes or any of them, and from time to time fix further meetings for the hearing and determining of objections, of which further meetings, when not holden by adjournment, notice shall be given in manner hereinbefore directed with regard to the original meeting; and when the said commissioners or assistant commissioner shall have heard and determined all such objections, they or he shall amend the draft of such award accordingly, if they or he shall see occasion. *Commissioners may hear and determine objections to the award.*

LII. And be it enacted, that as soon as the commissioners or assistant commissioner shall have made such amendments in the draft of the award as to them or him shall seem necessary, they or he shall cause the same to be fairly written, and shall sign and send it to the office of the commissioners, *Award to be confirmed by the commissioners.*

148 APPENDIX.

and the commissioners shall satisfy themselves that all the proceedings incident to the making of such award have been duly performed, and if they shall think that the award ought to be confirmed shall confirm the same under their hands and seal, and shall add to the award the date of such confirmation, and shall publish the fact of such confirmation and the date thereof in the parish, in such manner as to them shall seem fit; and every such confirmed award shall be binding on all persons interested in the said lands or tithes.

Commissioners to summon a parochial meeting to appoint valuers.

LIII. And be it enacted, that as soon as the commissioners shall have confirmed any such award, the commissioners or some assistant commissioner shall call a parochial meeting of the owners of land subject to tithes in the said parish, for the purpose of choosing valuers to apportion the amount so awarded among the lands of the parish, and shall give notice thereof in writing under their or his hand, to be fixed at least twenty-one days before such meeting on the principal outer door of the church or in some public and conspicuous place within the parish; and valuers or a single valuer may be chosen at such meeting by the land owners then present in like manner, and the valuers so chosen shall act with the same powers and be subject to the same provisions, as if the rent-charge so awarded had been agreed to at a parochial meeting of the land owners and tithe owners of the parish, and the valuers had been thereupon chosen as aforesaid.

If valuation not completed in six months, commissioners to apportion.

LIV. And be it enacted, that if upon the expiration of six calendar months after the day of the date of the confirmation of any agreement or award no valuer or valuers shall have been appointed, or the apportionment by such valuers or valuer shall not have been made and sent to the office of the commissioners as hereinafter provided, it shall be lawful for the commissioners or some assistant commissioner to apportion the rent-charge previously agreed or awarded to be paid among the lands of the said parish, having regard to the average titheable produce and productive quaility of the said lands, according to the discretion and judgment of the commissioners or assistant commissioner, but subject to the provisions hereinafter contained, and so that the several lands may have the full benefit in each case of every modus, composition real, prescriptive and customary payment, and of every exemption from or non-liability to tithes relating to the said lands respectively, and having regard to the several tithes to which the said lands are severally liable.

LV. And be it enacted, that a draft of every apportionment shall be made, and shall set forth the agreement or award, as the case may be, upon which such apportionment is founded, and every schedule thereunto annexed; and the said draft, or some schedule thereunto annexed, whether made by or under the direction of the valuers or commissioners or assistant commissioners, shall state the name or description and the true or estimated quantity in statute measure of the several lands to be comprised in the apportionment, and shall set forth the names and description of the several proprietors and occupiers thereof, and whether the said several lands are then cultivated as arable, meadow, or pasture land, or as wood land, common land, or howsoever otherwise, and shall refer, by a number set against the description of such lands, to a map or plan to be drawn on paper or parchment, and the same number shall be marked on the representation of such lands in the said map or plan; and the draft of the apportionment shall also state the amount charged upon the said several lands, and to whom and in what right the same shall be respectively payable. *Form of apportionment.*

LVI. And be it enacted, that immediately after the passing of this Act, and also in the month of January in every year, the comptroller of corn returns for the time being, or such other person as may from time to time be in that behalf authorised by the Privy Council, shall cause an advertisement to be inserted in the "London Gazette," stating what has been, during seven years ending on the Thursday next before Christmas day then next preceding, the average price of an imperial bushel of British wheat, barley, and oats, computed from the weekly averages of the corn returns. *Comptroller of corn returns to publish average price of corn.*

LVII. And be it enacted, that every rent-charge charged upon any lands by any such intended apportionment shall be deemed at the time of the confirmation of such apportionment, as hereinafter provided, to be of the value of such number of imperial bushels and decimal parts of an imperial bushel of wheat, barley, and oats, as the same would have purchased at the prices so ascertained by the advertisement to be published immediately after the passing of this Act, *Rent-charges to be valued according to the average price of corn.*

in case one third part of such rent-charge had been invested in the purchase of wheat, one third part thereof in the purchase of barley, and the remaining third part thereof in the purchase of oats, and the respective quantities of wheat, barley, and oats so ascertained shall be stated in the draft of every apportionment.

Rent-charge may be specially apportioned.

LVIII. And be it enacted, that it shall be lawful for the valuers or commissioners or any assistant commissioner, upon the request of any land owner, at any time before the confirmation of the apportionment, to apportion the whole rent-charge intended to be charged upon any lands of such land owner held under the same title and for the same estate, in the same parish, specially upon the several closes or portions of such lands or according to an acreable rate or acreable rates, upon lands of different quality, in such manner and in such proportion, and to the exclusion of such of them, as the land owner, with the consent of the person entitled to such rent-charge, may direct, and the particulars of every such special apportionment shall be included in the draft of the apportionment and taken to be a part thereof: provided always, that the extra expenses of every such special apportionment shall be borne by the party at whose instance the same shall have been made, and shall be recoverable as other costs of the apportionment are recoverable, and that no close of land shall be charged with any rent-charge or share of rent-charge on account of the tithes of any other lands, unless the value of such lands shall be at least three times the value of the whole rent-charge upon such lands.

Commissioners may employ surveyors.

LIX. And be it enacted, that for the purpose of making any such apportionment, as well as for the purpose of making any award as hereinbefore provided, the commissioners and assistant commissioners may employ such land surveyors and tithe valuers as to them shall seem fit, and may order them to be paid for valuing, surveying, mapping, and planning after any rate not exceeding two guineas to every such person for every day that he shall have been so employed, and may assess the same as part of the expenses of making their award or apportionment respectively; and the said commissioners and assistant commissioners, and the land survayers and tithe valuers employed by them respectively,

Commissioners to have the power of

shall have all the powers and be subject to all the provisions hereinbefore enacted concerning the valuers appointed at a parochial meeting, except that they shall not be bound to adopt any principles of apportionment agreed to at any parochial meeting: provided always, that it shall be lawful for such commissioners and assistant commissioners to make any agreement with any such land surveyors or tithe valuers for the payment to the same of one sum for the whole duty or any part thereof to be performed by them respectively.

valuers as to entry in lands, &c.

LX. And be it enacted, that the draft of every apportionment, whether made by or under the direction of the commissioners or any assistant commissioner, or by any valuer or valuers appointed as hereinbefore is provided, shall be signed by the person by or under whose direction it shall have been made, and shall be sent, together with the map or plan therein referred to, by the person by whom it is signed, to the office of the commissioners, or otherwise to some assistant commissioner, as the commissioners may direct, with such proof as the commissioners may require that every proceeding incident to the making of such draft of apportionment has been duly performed.

Apportionment to be signed by the person making it, and sent with the plan to the commissioners.

LXI. And be it enacted, that as soon as the draft of any such apportionment, verified as aforesaid, shall have been sent to the commissioners, they shall cause a copy of the same to be deposited at some convenient place within the said parish for the inspection of all persons interested in the said lands or tithes, and shall forthwith cause notice to be given, in such manner as to them shall seem fit, where the said copy may be inspected, and shall also in such notice appoint some convenient place and such times as they shall think necessary (the first not earlier than twenty-one days from the first giving of such notice) for holding a meeting to hear objections to the intended apportionment by any person interested therein, and the said commissioners or some assistant commissioner at such meeting as aforesaid shall hear and determine any objections which may be then and there made to the said intended apportionment, or adjourn the further hearing thereof, if they or he shall think proper, to a future meeting, and may, if they or he shall see occasion, direct any further valuation of the lands or any of

Commissioners may hear and determine objections to apportionment.

them, and from time to time fix further meetings for the hearing and determining of objections, of which further meetings, when not holden by adjournment, notice shall be given in manner hereinbefore directed with regard to the original meeting; and when the said commissioners or assistant commissioner shall have heard and determined all such objections, they and he are and is hereby required to cause such apportionment to be amended accordingly if they or he shall see occasion.

Owners of lands chargeable with rent-charge may give land instead thereof.

LXII. And be it enacted, that it shall be lawful for the owner of any lands chargeable with any such rent-charge to agree, at any time before the confirmation of any such instrument of apportionment, with any ecclesiastical person being the owner of the tithes thereof in right of any spiritual benefice or dignity, for giving land instead of the rent-charge charged or about to be charged upon his lands; and every such agreement shall be made under the hands and seals of the land owner and tithe owner, and shall contain all the particulars hereinbefore required to be inserted in a parochial agreement for giving land instead of tithes or rent-charge: provided always, that no such tithe owner shall be enabled to take or hold more than twenty imperial acres of land in the whole by virtue of any such agreement or agreements made in the same parish; and the same consent and confirmation relatively to the lands and tithes comprised in the said agreement shall be necessary to any such agreement as in the case of a parochial agreement for giving land instead of tithes; and all the provisions hereinbefore contained concerning a parochial agreement for giving land shall be applicable to every such agreement, as hereinbefore last mentioned, so far as concerns the lands and tithes comprised in the said agreement: provided also, that any amendment which shall be made in the draft of apportionment before confirmation thereof, and subsequent to any such agreement for giving land instead of rent-charge, whereby the charge upon the lands referred to in such agreement shall be altered, shall be taken to annul the execution of such agreement for giving land, and any consent which may have been necessary thereunto.

Confirmation by the

LXIII. And be it enacted, that after such proceedings as

aforesaid shall have been had, and all such objections, if any, shall have been finally disposed of, the commissioners or assistant commissioner shall cause the instrument of apportionment to be engrossed on parchment, and shall annex the map or plan thereunto belonging to the engrossed instrument of apportionment, and shall sign the instrument of apportionment and the map or plan, and shall send both to the office of the commissioners, and if the commissioners shall approve the apportionment they shall confirm the instrument of apportionment under their hands and seal, and shall add thereunto the date of such confirmation. Commissioners.

LXIV. And be it enacted, that two copies of every confirmed instrument of apportionment, and of every confirmed agreement for giving land instead of any tithes or rent-charge, shall be made and sealed with the seal of the said commissioners, and one such copy shall be deposited in the registry of the diocese within which the parish is situated, to be there kept among the records of the said registry, and the other copy shall be deposited with the incumbent and church or chapel wardens of the parish for the time being, or such other fit persons as the commissioners shall approve, to be kept by them and their successors in office with the public books, writings, and papers of the parish; and all persons interested therein may have access to and be furnished with copies of or extracts from any such copy on giving reasonable notice to the person having custody of the same, and on payment of two shillings and sixpence for such inspection, and after the rate of threepence for every seventy-two words contained in such copy or extract; and every recital or statement in or map or plan annexed to such confirmed apportionment or agreement for giving land, or any sealed copy thereof, shall be deemed satisfactory evidence of the matters therein recited or stated, or of the accuracy of such plan. Transcripts of the award to be sent to the registrar of the diocese and to the incumbent and churchwardens.

LXV. And be it enacted, that the commissioners, if they shall see fit, before confirming any agreement, award, or apportionment, may require notice thereof to be given in such manner as they shall direct to the person next in remainder, reversion, or expectancy of an estate of inheritance in any lands or tithes, or any other person to whom they Commissioners may require notice of agreements or awards to be given to reversioner.

may think notice ought to be given, and may by themselves or by some assistant commissioner hear and determine any objection made to such confirmation by any person interested therein, and may direct any award or apportionment to be amended accordingly.

<small>Agreements, &c. not to be questioned after confirmation.</small>

LXVI. And be it enacted, that no confirmed agreement, award, or apportionment shall be impeached after the confirmation thereof by reason of any mistake or informality therein or in any proceeding relating thereunto.

<small>Lands to be discharged from tithes, and rent-charge paid in lieu thereof.</small>

LXVII. And be it enacted, that from the first day of January next following the confirmation of every such apportionment the lands of the said parish shall be absolutely discharged from the payment of all tithes, except so far as relates to the liability of any tenant at rack rent dissenting as hereinafter provided, and instead thereof there shall be payable thenceforth to the person in that behalf mentioned in the said apportionment a sum of money equal in value, according to the prices ascertained by the then next preceding advertisement, to the quantity of wheat, barley, and oats respectively mentioned therein to be payable instead of the said tithes, in the nature of a rent-charge issuing out of the lands charged therewith; and such yearly sum shall be payable by two equal half-yearly payments on the first day of July and the first day of January in every year, the first payment, except in the case of barren reclaimed lands, as hereinafter provided, being on the first day of July next after the lands shall have been discharged from tithes as aforesaid; and such rent-charge may be recovered at the suit of the person entitled thereto, his executors or adminitrators, by distress and entry as hereinafter mentioned; and after every first day of January the sum of money thenceforth payable in respect of such rent-charge shall vary so as always to consist of the price of the same number of bushels and decimal parts of a bushel of wheat, barley, and oats respectively, according to the prices ascertained by the then next preceding advertisement, and any person entitled from time to time to any such varied rent-charge shall have the same powers for enforcing payment thereof as are herein contained concerning the original rent-charge: provided always, that nothing herein contained shall be taken to render any person whomsoever personally liable to the payment of any such rent-charge: provided always, that the rent-charge which shall be apportioned upon any lands in the said parish which during any part of the said period of seven years preceding Christmas one thousand eight hundred and thirty-five were exmpted from tithes by reason of having been enclosed under any Act of Parliament, or converted from barren heath or waste ground, shall be payable for the first time on the first day of July or first day of January next following the confirmation of the apportionment which shall be nearest to the time at which tithes were or would have become payable for the first time in respect of the said ands if no commutation thereof had taken place. Payment of rent-charge on reclaimed lands to be postponed until tithes would have been due.

LXVIII. And be it enacted, that from the first day of January next following the confirmation of every parochial or other agreement for giving land instead of any tithes or rent-charge, the lands of the parish in which any such agreement shall be made shall be absolutely discharged from the payment of the tithes or rent-charge for which it shall have been agreed that such land shall be given. Lands to be free from tithes when lands are given in lieu thereof.

LXIX. And be it enacted, that every rent-charge payable as aforesaid instead of tithes shall be subject to all parliamentary, parochial, and county and other rates, charges, and assessments, in like manner as the tithes commuted for such rent-charge have heretofore been subject. Rent-charge to be liable to parochial and county rates.

LXX. And be it enacted, that all rates and charges to which any such rent-charge is liable shall be assessed upon the occupier of the lands out of which such rent-charge shall issue, and in case the same shall not be sooner paid by the owner of the rent-charge for the time being may be recovered from such occupier in like manner as any poor rate assessed on him in respect of such lands; and any occupier holding such lands under any landlord, and who shall have paid any such rate or charge in respect of any such rent-charge, shall be entitled to deduct the amount thereof from the rent next payable by him to his landlord for the time being, and shall be allowed the same in account with his landlord; and any landlord or owner in possession who shall have paid any such rate or charge, or from whose rent the amount of any such rate or charge in respect of any such rent-charge shall have How rates and charges are to be recovered.

been so deducted, or who shall have allowed the same in account with any tenant paying the same, shall be entitled to deduct the amount thereof from the rent-charge, or by all other lawful ways and means to recover the same from the owner of the rent-charge, his executors and administrators; provided that the owner of every such rent-charge shall have and be entitled to the like right of demanding, inspecting, and taking copies of every assessment containing such rate or charge, and of appeal against the same, and the like power of prosecuting such appeal, and the like remedies in respect thereof, as any occupier or rate-payer has or may have in the case of poor rates, although such rate or charge is herein made assessable upon the occupier, and the owner of the rent-charge is not mentioned by name in such assessment.

Rent-charge to be subject to the same incumbrances and incidents as tithe before this Act.

LXXI. And be it enacted, that any person having any interest in or claim to any tithes, or to any charge or incumbrance upon any tithes, before the passing of this Act, shall have the same right to or claim upon the rent-charge for which the same shall be commuted as he had to or upon the tithes, and shall be entitled to have the like remedies for recovering the same as if his right or claim to or upon the rent-charge had accrued after the commutation; provided that nothing herein contained shall give validity to any mortgage or other incumbrance which before the passing of this Act was invalid or could not be enforced; and every estate for life, or other greater estate, in any such rent-charge shall be taken to be an estate of freehold; and every estate in any such rent-charge shall be subject to the same liabilities and incidents as the like estate in the tithes commuted for such rent-charge; and where any lands were exempted from tithe whilst in the occupation of the owner thereof by reason of being glebe or of having been heretofore parcel of the possessions of any privileged order, the same lands shall be in like manner exempted from the payment of the rent-charge apportioned on them whilst in the occupation of the owner thereof; and where by virtue of any Act or Acts of Parliament heretofore passed any tithes are authorised to be sold, exchanged, appropriated, or applied in any way, the rent-charges for which such tithes may be commuted under the provisions of this Act, or any part thereof, shall or may be saleable or exchangeable, appropriated and applied, to all intents and purposes, in like manner as such tithes, and the same powers of sale, exchange, and appropriation shall in all such cases extend to and may be exercised in respect of the said commutation rent-charges; and the money to arise by the sale of such rent-charges shall or may be invested, appropriated, and applied to the same purposes and in like manner as the money to arise by the sale of any such tithes might have been invested, appropriated, and applied under such particular Act or Acts in case this Act had not been passed; and no such rent-charge shall merge or be extinguished in any estate of which the person for the time being entitled to such rent-charge may be seised or possessed in the lands on which the same shall be charged: provided always, that it shall be lawful for any person seised in possession of an estate in fee simple or fee tail of any tithes, or rent-charge in lieu of tithes, by any deed or declaration under his hand and seal, to be made in such form as the said commissioners shall approve, and to be confirmed under their seal, to release, assign, or otherwise dispose of the same, so that the same may be absolutely merged and extinguished in the freehold and inheritance of the lands on which the same shall have been charged. *Proviso.*

LXXII. And be it enacted, that if at any time subsequent to the confirmation of any such instrument of apportionment the owner of any lands charged with any such rent-charge shall be desirous that the apportionment thereof shall be altered, it shall be lawful for the commissioners of land tax for the county or place where the said lands are situate, or any three of them, to alter the apportionment in such manner and in such proportion and to the exclusion of such of the lands as the land owner, with the consent of two justices of the peace acting for the county, riding, division, or other jurisdiction in which the lands are situated, may direct; and such altered apportionment shall be made by an instrument in writing under the hands and seals of the said commissioners of land tax and of the said land owner and justices, of the like form and tenor as to the said lands as the original apportionment, and bearing date the day of its execution by the said commissioners of land tax, subject to the provision *Apportionment may be altered by commissioners of land tax, if desired.*

hereinbefore contained with respect to the value of lands on which any rent-charge may be charged on account of the tithes of any other lands; and every such altered apportionment shall be as valid as if made and confirmed by the tithe commissioners as aforesaid, and shall be taken to be an amendment of the original apportionment; and in every such case two counterparts of the instrument of altered apportionment, under the hands and seals of the said commissioners of land tax and justices and land owner, shall be sent, one to the registrar of the diocese, and one to the incumbent and church or chapel wardens, or other person having the custody of the other copy of the original instrument of apportionment; and one counterpart shall be annexed to the copy of the instrument of apportionment in the custody of the registrar and such other person respectively, and taken to be an amendment thereof; and thenceforward such lands shall be charged only according to such altered apportionment; and all expenses of such alteration shall be borne by the land owner desiring the same.

Expenses of witnesses to be paid under the direction of the commissioners.

LXXIII. And be it enacted, that the commissioners or assistant commissioner, in any case where they or he may see fit, may order such expenses of witnesses, and of the production of any books, deeds, contracts, agreements, accounts, or writings, terriers, maps, plans, and surveys, or copies thereof, and all other expenses (except the salary or allowance to any commissioner or assistant commissioner) incurred in the settlement of any suit or difference, or in the hearing and determining any objection to any award or apportionment before the said commissioners or any assistant commissioner, to be paid by such parties interested in the production thereof respectively or in the event of such suit, difference, or objection, and in such proportions, as the commissioners or assistant commissioners shall think fit and reasonable.

Expenses of making any award to be paid by the land owners and tithe owners as the commissioners may direct.

LXXIV. And be it enacted, the allowances to and expenses of land surveyors and tithe valuers necessary for making any award, and all other expenses of or incident to making the said award, except the salary or allowance to any commissioner or assistant commissioner, and except any expenses which the commissioners or any assistant commissioner, or any court or arbitrator, may be authorised to order and may have ordered to be otherwise paid, shall be borne and paid by the land owners and tithe owners interested in the said award, in such proportion, time, and manner as the commissioners or assistant commissioner shall direct.

LXXV. And be it enacted, that all the expenses of or incident to making any apportionment (except the salary or allowance to any commissioner or assistant commissioner, and except any expense which the commissioners or assistant commissioner may be authorised and may have ordered to be otherwise paid) shall be borne and paid by the owners of lands included in the apportionment in rateable proportion to the sum charged on the said lands in lieu of tithes by such apportionment. *Expenses of apportionment to be borne rateably by the land owners.*

LXXVI. And be it enacted, that if any difference shall arise touching the said expenses, or the share thereof to be paid by any person, it shall be lawful for the commissioners or some assistant commissioner to certify under their or his hand the amount to be paid by such person; and in case any person shall neglect or refuse to pay his share so certified to be payable by him, and upon the production of such certificate before any two justices of the peace for the county or other jurisdiction wherein the lands mentioned in the agreement or award or apportionment are situate, such justices, upon the nonpayment thereof, are hereby required, by warrant under their hands and seals, to cause the same and the costs of the distress to be levied by distress and sale of the goods of the person liable to pay the same, and to render the surplus (if any), after deducting the charges of the distress and sale, to the person distrained upon. *Expenses may be recovered by warrant of distress.*

LXXVII. And be it enacted, that every owner of an estate in land or tithes less in the whole than an immediate estate of fee simple or fee tail, or which shall be settled upon any uses or trusts, may, with the consent of the commissioners, and in such manner as they may direct, charge so much of the expenses of commutation as is to be defrayed by him, or any part thereof, and the interest thereon after the rate of four pounds by the hundred, upon the lands whereof the tithes are commuted, or upon the rent-charge to be received by him instead of such tithes respectively, but so nevertheless that the charges upon such lands or rent-charge *Owners of particular estates may charge the costs on the estate for twenty years.*

respectively shall be lessened in every year following such commutation by one twentieth part at least of the whole original charge thereon.

<small>Costs of ecclesiastical tithe owners may be charged on the benefice for twenty years.</small>

LXXVIII. And be it enacted, that every ecclesiastical beneficed person who shall commute the tithes of his benefice under this Act may advance or borrow the sum necessary to defray so much of the expenses of commutation as is to be defrayed by him, or any part thereof, and as a security for repayment may charge or assign the rent-charge to be received instead of such tithes for twenty years, or until the principal sum advanced or borrowed, and the interest thereon after the rate of four pounds by the hundred, and the expenses of such charge or assignment, shall be sooner paid; and every incumbent successively shall pay the interest of the sum advanced or borrowed, or of so much thereof as shall then remain unpaid, as the same shall become due, or within one calendar month next following, and also an instalment at the rate of five pounds for every hundred pounds of the principal sum advanced or borrowed, and in default of such payment the ordinary may sequester the profits of the benefice until such payments shall be made, provided that the sum to be so advanced or borrowed shall be ascertained and certified under the hand of any commissioner or assistant commissioner, and shall be by him stated to have been the amount of such expenses properly incurred by such ecclesiastical beneficed person in relation to such commutation.

<small>If tenant of lands at rack rent dissent from paying the rent-charge, the landlord may take the tithes during the tenancy.</small>

LXXIX. And be it enacted, that any tenant or occupier who at the time of such commutation shall occupy at rack rent any lands of which the tithes shall be so commuted may, within one calendar month next after the confirmation of the appointment by the commissioners, signify, by writing under his hand given to or left at the usual residence of his landlord or his agent, his dissent from being bound to pay any rent-charge apportioned and charged on the said lands as aforesaid, and in that case such landlord shall be entitled, from the time when the said apportionment shall take effect, and during the tenancy or occupation of such tenant or occupier, to stand, as to the perception and collection of tithes or receipt of any composition instead thereof, in the place of the owner of the tithes so commuted, and to have all the powers and remedies for enforcing render and payment of such tithes or composition which the tithe owner would have had if the commutation had not taken place.

LXXX. And be it enacted, that any tenant or occupier at the time of such commutation who shall have signified his dissent from being bound to pay any such rent-charge as aforesaid, or who shall hold his lands under a lease or agreement providing that the same shall be holden and enjoyed by him free of tithes, and every tenant or occupier who shall occupy any lands by any lease or agreement made subsequently to such commutation, and who shall pay any such rent-charge, shall be entitled to deduct the amount thereof from the rent payable by him to his landlord, and shall be allowed the same in account with the said landlord. *Tenant paying rent-charge to be allowed the same in account with his landlord.*

LXXXI. And be it enacted, that in case the said rent-charge shall at any time be in arrear and unpaid for the space of twenty-one days next after any half-yearly day of payment, it shall be lawful for the person entitled to the same, after having given or left ten days' notice in writing at the usual or last known residence of the tenant in possession, to distrain upon the lands liable to the payment thereof, or on any part thereof, for all arrears of the said rent-charge, and to dispose of the distress when taken, and otherwise to act and demean himself in relation thereto as any landlord may for arrears of rent reserved on a common lease for years; provided that not more than two years' arrears shall at any time be recoverable by distress. *When rent-charge is in arrear for twenty-one days after half-yearly days of payment, the person entitled thereto may distrain.*

LXXXII. And be it enacted, that in case the said rent-charge shall be in arrear and unpaid for the space of forty days next after any half-yearly day of payment, and there shall be no sufficient distress on the premises liable to the payment thereof, it shall be lawful for any judge of his Majesty's courts of record at Westminster, upon affidavit of the facts, to order a writ to be issued, directed to the sheriff of the county in which the lands chargeable with the rent-charge are situated, requiring the said sheriff to summon a jury to assess the arrears of rent-charge remaining unpaid, and to return the inquisition thereupon taken to some one of his Majesty's courts of law at Westminster, on a day therein to be named, either in term time or vacation; a copy of *When rent-charges are in arrear for forty days after half-yearly days of payment, and no sufficient distress on the premises, writ to be issued directing sheriff to summon jury to assess arrears.*

M

which writ, and notice of the time and place of executing the same, shall be given to the owner of the land, or left at his last known place of abode, or with his known agent, ten days previous to the execution thereof; and the sheriff is hereby required to execute such writ according to the exigency thereof; and the costs of such inquisition shall be taxed by the proper officer of the court; and thereupon the owner of the rent-charge may sue out a writ of habere facias possessionem, directed to the sheriff, commanding him to cause the owner of the rent-charge to have possession of the lands chargeable therewith until the arrears of rent-charge found to be due, and the said costs, and also the costs of such writ and of executing the same, and of cultivating and keeping possession of the lands, shall be fully satisfied: provided always, that not more than two years' arrears over and above the time of such possession shall be at any time recoverable.

<small>Account how to be rendered.</small>

LXXXIII. And be it enacted, that it shall be lawful for the court out of which such writ shall have issued, or any judge at chambers, to order the owner of the rent-charge who shall be in possession by virtue of such writ from time to time to render an account of the rents and produce of the lands and of the receipts and payments in respect of the same, and to pay over the surplus (if any) to the person for the time being entitled thereunto, after satisfaction of such arrears of rent-charge and all costs and expenses as aforesaid, and thereupon to order a writ of supersedeas to issue to the said writ of habere facias possessionem, and also by rule or order of such court or judge from time to time to give such summary relief to the parties as to the said court or judge shall seem fit.

<small>For recovery of rent-charges from Quakers.</small>

LXXXIV. Provided always, and be it enacted, that in all cases in which it shall be necessary to make any distress under this Act in respect of any lands in the possession of any person of the persuasion of the people called Quakers, the same may be made upon the goods, chattels, or effects of such person, whether on the premises or elsewhere, but nevertheless to the same amount only and with the same consequences in all respects as if made on the premises; and that in all cases of distress under this Act upon persons of that persuasion the goods, chattels, or effects which may be distrained shall be sold without its being necessary to impound or keep the same: provided always, that no writ under the provision hereinbefore contained shall be issued for assessing or recovering any rent-charge payable under this Act in respect of any lands in the possession of any person of the persuasion aforesaid, unless the same shall be in arrear and unpaid for the space of forty days next after any half-yearly day of payment, without the person entitled thereto being able to find goods, chattels, or effects, either on the premises or elsewhere liable to be distrained as aforesaid sufficient to satisfy the arrears to which such lands are liable, together with the reasonable costs of such distress.

LXXXV. And be it enacted, that whenever any rent-charge payable under the provisions of this Act shall be in arrear, notwithstanding any apportionment which may have been made of any such rent-charge, every part of the land situate in the parish in which such rent-charge shall so be in arrear, and which shall be occupied by the same person who shall be the occupier of the lands on which such rent-charge so in arrear shall have been charged, whether such land shall be occupied by the person occupying the same as the owner thereof, or as tenant thereof, holding under the same landlord under whom he occupies the land on which such rent-charge so in arrear shall have been charged, shall be liable to be distrained upon or entered upon as aforesaid for the purpose of satisfying any arrears of such rent-charge, whether chargeable on the lands on which such distress is taken or such entry made, or upon any other part of the lands so occupied or holden: provided always, that no land shall be liable to be distrained or entered upon for the purpose of satisfying any such rent-charge charged upon lands which shall have been washed away by the sea, or otherwise destroyed by any natural casualty. *Powers of distress and entry to extend to all lands within the parish occupied by the owner or under the same landlord or holding.*

LXXXVI. And be it enacted, that the several provisions of an Act passed in the fourth and fifth years of his present Majesty, intituled " An Act to amend an Act of the eleventh year of King George the Second, respecting the apportionment of rents, annuities, and other periodical payments," shall extend to all rent-charges payable under this Act. *Powers of 4 & 5 W. 4. to extend to rent-charges under this Act.*

Provision for the sale of buildings and the sites thereof rendered useless or unnecessary by the commutation of tithes.

LXXXVII. And be it enacted, that if any barns or buildings belonging to any tithe owner having a limited estate or interest therein, which shall have been generally used for the housing of tithes paid in kind, shall be rendered in the whole or in part useless by reason of any commutation of tithes under this Act, it shall be lawful for every such tithe owner (with the consent, nevertheless, of the commissioners, and subject to such directions as they may give, to be signified under their hands and seal) to pull down any such barns or buildings or any part thereof, and to sell and dispose of the materials, or to sell and dispose of all or any of such barns or buildings, and the site thereof, and either with or without any farm buildings or homesteads thereunto belonging, in such manner as the commissioners may direct; and upon payment of the consideration money it shall be lawful for every such tithe owner (with such consent as aforesaid) to convey and deliver the premises sold as aforesaid to the purchaser thereof, or to such uses and in such manner as such purchaser shall direct; and the consideration money in each case shall be paid to such tithe owner, and his receipt shall be a good discharge to the purchaser; and such tithe owner shall lay out and invest the consideration money in such manner and for such trusts as the commissioners shall direct, for the benefit of the persons entitled to the said rent-charge.

Leases of tithes may be surrendered.

LXXXVIII. And be it enacted, that it shall be lawful for the lessee being in occupation of any tithes commuted under this Act, by an instrument in writing under his hand and seal, to be made in such form as the commissioners shall direct, and confirmed under their seal, to surrender and make void the lease by which the said tithes are held or enjoyed by such lessee at the time of the commutation, so far as the same may relate to the said tithes; and it shall be lawful for the commissioners by the same instrument to direct what compensation (if any) shall be given by the immediate lessor of any lessee at rack rent so surrendering any lease of any such tithes to such lessee, and what allowance (if any) shall be made by any lessee to his immediate lessor of any such surrendered lease, in consideration of the non-fulfilment of any conditions contained in such lease, and what deduction (if any) shall be made from the rent thenceforth payable by any lessee to his immediate lessor in respect of other hereditaments which may have been included with the said tithes in any such lease: provided always, that any intermediate lessor to whom any such lease shall have been surrendered shall as regards his immediate lessor be taken to be the lessee in occupation of the tithes included in the said lease.

LXXXIX. And be it enacted, that nothing in this Act contained shall affect any right to any tithes which shall have become due before the commutation. *Tithes due before commutation not to be affected.*

XC. And be it enacted, that nothing in this Act contained, unless by special provision to be inserted in some parochial agreement and specially approved by the commissioners, in which case the same shall be valid, shall extend to any Easter offerings, mortuaries, or surplice fees, or to the tithes of fish or of fishing, or to any personal tithes other than the tithes of mills, or any mineral tithes, or to any payment instead of tithes arising or growing due within the city of London, or to any permanent rent-charge or other rent or payment in lieu of tithes, calculated according to any rate or proportion in the pound on the rent or value of any houses or lands in any city or town under any custom or private Act of Parliament, or to any lands or tenements the tithes whereof shall have been already perpetually commuted or extinguished under any Act of Parliament heretofore made. *Act not to extend to Easter offerings, &c., or to payments instead of tithes in London, or to permanent rent-charges by custom or Act of Parliament.*

XCI. And be it enacted, that no advertisement inserted by direction of the commissioners or any assistant commissioner, or by any tithe owner or land owner, in the "London Gazette," or in any newspaper, for the purpose of carrying into effect any provision of this Act, and no agreement, award, or power of attorney made or confirmed or used under this Act, shall be chargeable with any stamp duty. *Advertisements, contracts, and awards not to be liable to stamp duty.*

XCII. And be it enacted, that the said commissioners may receive and send by the General Post from and to places in England and Wales all letters and packets relating exclusively to the execution of this Act free from the duty of postage, provided that such letters and packets as shall be *Corespondence of commissioners relating to this Act to be free of postage.*

sent to the said commissioners be directed to the " Tithe Commissioners for England and Wales," at their office in London, and that all such letters and packets as shall be sent by the said commissioners shall be in covers, with the words "Tithe Commissioners for England and Wales" printed on the same, and be signed on the outside thereof under such words with the name of such person in his own handwriting as the said commissioners, with the consent of the lords commissioners of the treasury or any three or more of them, shall appoint (such name to be from time to time sent to the secretary of the General Post Office in London), and be sealed with the seal of the said commissioners, and under such other regulations as the said lords commissioners or any three or more of them shall think fit; and if the person so to be appointed shall subscribe or seal any letter or packet whatever, except such only concerning which he shall receive the special direction of his superior officer, or which he shall himself know to relate exclusively to the execution of this Act, or if the person so to be appointed, or any other person, shall send or cause to be sent under any such cover any letter, paper, or writing, or any inclosure, other than shall relate exclusively to the execution of this Act, every person so offending shall forfeit and pay the sum of one hundred pounds and be dismissed from his office, one moiety of such penalty shall be paid to the use of his Majesty, his heirs and successors, and the other moiety to the use of the person who shall inform or sue for the same; and every such penalty may be sued for and recovered in any of his Majesty's courts of record in Westminster.

False evidence to be deemed perjury; withholding evidence a misdemeanour. XCIII. And be it enacted, that if any person under the provisions of this Act shall wilfully give false evidence he shall be deemed guilty of perjury; and if any person shall make or subscribe a false affidavit or declaration for the purposes of this Act he shall suffer the penalties of perjury; and if any person shall wilfully refuse to attend in obedience to any lawful summons of any commissioner or assistant commissioner, or to give evidence, or shall wilfully alter, withhold, destroy, or refuse to produce any book, deed, contract, agreement, account, or writing, terrier, map, plan, or survey, or any copy of the same, which may be lawfully required to be produced before the said commissioners or assistant commissioner, he shall be deemed guilty of a misdemeanor.

XCIV. And be it enacted, that no action or suit shall be commenced against any commissioner, assistant commissioner, justice of the peace, valuer, umpire, or surveyor, for anything done under the authority of this Act, until twenty-one days' notice thereof shall have been given in writing to the party against whom such action or suit is intended to be brought, or after sufficient satisfaction or tender of amends shall have been made to any party aggrieved, or after three calendar months shall have expired from the commission of the act for which such action or suit shall be so brought; and every such action shall be brought, laid, and tried in the county or place where the cause of action shall have arisen, and not in any other county or place; and if it shall appear that such notice of action or suit was brought before twenty-one days' notice thereof given as aforesaid, or that sufficient amends were made or tendered as aforesaid, or if any such action or suit shall not be commenced within the time before limited in that behalf, or such action shall be laid in any county or place other than as aforesaid, then the jury shall find a verdict for the defendant therein, or the court, upon summary application by motion in any such suit, may dismiss the same against such defendant; and if a verdict shall be found for such defendant, or such suit shall be dismissed upon application as aforesaid, or if the plaintiff in such action or suit shall become nonsuit, or suffer a discontinuance of such action, or if upon any demurrer in such action or suit judgment shall be given for the defendant therein, then such defendant shall have costs, charges, and expenses as between attorney and client.

Limitation of actions against commissioners, assistant commissioners, justices, &c.

XCV. And be it enacted, that no order, adjudication, or proceeding made or had by or before the commissioners or any assistant commissioner under the authority of this Act, or any proceeding to be had touching any offender against this Act, shall be quashed for want of form, or be removed or removable by certiorari, or any other writ or process,

Proceedings under this Act not to be quashed for want of form, nor to be removed by certiorari.

into any of his Majesty's courts of record at Westminster or elsewhere.

Limits of Act. XCVI. And be it enacted, that this Act shall extend only to England and Wales.

Act may be altered this session. XCVII. And be it further enacted, that this Act may be amended, altered, or repealed by any Act or Acts to be passed in this present session of Parliament.

INDEX.

Aelstan's conspiracy against Ethelwolf, 17.
Agistment, tithes of, how levied, 42.
Agobard, his testimony respecting the support of the Church, 10.
Alfred's law of tithes, 20, 36.
Althorp, Lord, on Church property, 112.
Anglo-Saxon Church, revenues of, how administered, *note*, 70.
Animals, tithes of, how levied, 49.
Appropriations, establishment and increase of, 73; extent of, 74; secured by special deed, 75; characteristics of these deeds, 75–77; specimen of instrument of appropriation, 77; appropriations do not alter compulsory origin of parochial tithes, 78; were always from a Church, not to it, 79; granted to laymen by the statutes of dissolution, 80.
Arbitrary consecrations of tithes, 65; proofs of, from Pope Innocent III., Wickliffe, Lord Chancellor Parning, Judges Ludlow and Brooke, and Dyer and Selden, 67, 68; effects of, on tithe endowments, 70.
Articles, the thirty-nine, prescribed by the State, *note*, 93.
Athelstan's law of tithes, 22.
Ayliffe, on the origin of tithes, 117.

Barren land, law of tithes of, 57; legal definition of, *note*, 62.
Bishops, their homage for their temporalities, 90.
Brougham, Lord, on Church property being national property, *note*, 98; on the Church not a corporation, 106.
Caird's estimate of land under cultivation, 56.
Calchuth, council of, 15.

Campbell, Lord, on Church property, 110.
Canute's law of tithes, 24, 36.
Charlemagne's laws of tithes, 11.
Chaucer on tithes, 35.
Church, early Christian, knew nothing of tithes, 7; mode of its support, 7, 8.
Church of England, the phrase defined, 1, 2, *note*, 84, 95; holds no property in her own right, 85; has no corporate rights to religious endowments, 91; not distinguishable from the whole people, 95; not a corporation, 105, 106.
Church property always dealt with as the property of the State, 84–102; not of one kind, 104.
Church rates, probable origin of, 81-83.
Church-scot, *note*, 22.
Clergy, early encroachments of the, 30, 66; are servants of the State, 107.
Commons, the, complaints of against the clergy, 32, *note*, 41.
Corn and grain, tithes of, how levied, 39.

Danes, the, effects of their invasions, 28.
Dissolution, statutes of, *note*, 87.

Eastern Church has never resorted to tithes, 9.
Edgar's law of tithes, 23.
Edinburgh Review, on the Church not a corporation, 106; on Church property, 113.
Egbert, Archbishop of York, canons of, 14.
Eggs, tithes of, how levied, 50.
Eldon, Lord, on Church-membership, *note*, 96.
Enclosure Bills, number passed from

1760 to 1849, 56; number of acres enclosed by ditto, 57.
Endowments, parochial, see Tithes.
England, condition of in the middle ages, 28; ditto in the seventeenth century, 62, 63.
England and Wales, extent of land under cultivation in, 55.
Ethelred's law of tithes, 23.
Ethelwolf's law of tithes, 23.
Extra-parochial tithes belonged to the Crown, 60, 88.

Fee-simple of Church property is in the State, 101.
Fish, tithes of, how levied, 51.
Flax, tithes of, how levied, 46.
Fruit, tithes of, how levied, 44.
Fuller, on origin of tithes in England, 116.

Gregory, Pope, on the division of ecclesiastical revenues, *note*, 31.
Guntheram reigning when tithes were first established, 9.
Guthrun's treaty with Alfred, 21.

Hardwicke, Lord, on the clergy as servants of the State, 107.
Hay, tithes of, how levied, 40.
Hemp, tithes of, how levied, 46.
Herbs, tithes of, how levied, 44.
Honey, tithes of, how levied, 46.
Hooker on Church-membership, *note*, 95.
Hops, tithes of, how levied, 46.

Ingulph's version of Ethelwolf's grant of tithes, 18.

Jurisdiction of ecclesiastical causes in Anglo-Saxon times, *note*, 88.

Lay recusancy in regard to tithes, 27.

Macaulay, Lord, on Church property, 112.
Mackintosh, Sir J., on the priesthood not being the proprietors of Church property, *note*, 97, 108—111.
Maçon, council of, 9; reasons for discrediting it, *note*, 10.
M'Culloch's estimate of land under cultivation, 56.
Marculphus's collection of deeds, &c., 11.
Melbourne, Lord, on Church property, 111.
Milk, tithes of, how levied, 48.
Mills, tithes of, how levied, 51.
Milman, Dean, on the origin of tithes, 113.

Mixed tithes, what they comprised, 47
Monasteries, suppression of by Henry VIII., 85.

Offa, his character, 15; his law of tithes, 16, 17.

Palmerston, Lord, on Church property, 112.
Parish church, legal characteristics of, *note*, 70.
Parishes formed since adoption of tithes, 61.
Parliament, its right to deal with Church property, 5.
Parochial endowments originated in public law, 100.
Parsons, rights of, respecting parochial endowments, 91.
Pepin's grant of tithes, 11.
Personal tithes, what they comprised, 50.
Pigeons, tithes of, how levied, 50.
Plough alms, *note*, 22.
Population of England and Wales A.D. 1575, 58; ditto, A.D. 1377, 59; ditto, A.D. 1200, 59.
Poultry, tithes of, how levied, 50.
Prædial tithes great, what they comprised, 39; ditto, small, 42.
Protestant Episcopalians have no especial claim on Church property, 98, 99.

Rent-charges, in lieu of tithes, 4.
Robertson, Rev. J. C., on tithes, 114.

Seeds, tithes of, how levied, 47.
Selden on the public origin of tithes, 104.
Services, Church, prescribed by the State, 92, 93.
State, the, constitutional right of to deal with Church property, 85–102.
Stephen, charter of, *note*, 25; law respecting tithes, 27.
Stillingfleet on the origin of tithes, 117.

Taylor, Rev. I., on Church property, 118.
Temporalities of bishops held from the Crown, 90.
Tertullian on the support of the early Church, *note*, 7.
Theophilact, legate of Hadrian I., 16.
Tithe Crimination Act, APPENDIX, 121; operation of, 4.
Tithes not in existence in the early Christian Church, 7; first opinion respecting them, 8; claimed on behalf of the poor, *ib.*; not claimed by the Eastern Church, 9; payment of,

INDEX. 171

ordained at the Council of Maçon, *ib.*; first general law for their payment, 11; royal consecrations of, ib.; made compulsory by Charlemagne, 11, 12; the law inoperative, 12, 13.

Tithes, parochial, they are the principal provision for the support of the Church, 4; origin of, in England, 14–17; law of Offa, 17; law of Ethelwolf, 17–20; this law the origin of the civil right to tithes, 20; laws of Alfred, 20, 21; law of Athelstan, 22; law of Edgar, 23; law of Ethelred, 23; law of Canute, 24; law of William I., 24; oath of Henry I., Stephen, and Henry II., 25; lay recusancy, 27; remarks on the re-enactments of the law, 29; original quadripartite division of tithes, 31; tripartite division, 31; laws of Henry VIII., *note*, 33; law necessary to enforce them. 34; fines and penalties for non-payment of, 35–37; things legally titheable, 38–52; observations on ditto, 52; always dealt with as originating in law, 52, 53; derived from the soil, 55; one-third of the titheable property brought into cultivation within the last century, 57; three-fourths within 300 years, 58; nine-tenths traceable to public law, 59; title to modern tithes not given by original landowners, 60; extra-parochial tithes belonged to the Crown, 61; absurdity of the private theory, 63; arbitrary assignments of tithes, 65–69; effects of these assignments, 69; mode of distributing tithe by lay owners, 71; appropriations, 73; appropriated tithes secured by deed, 75; general character of instruments of appropriation, 75–77; copy of instrument of appropriation, 77–78; arbitrary consecrations do not alter compulsory origin, 78; they were always from a church, not to it, 79; appropriated tithes granted to laymen, 80; all these now secularised, 81; now commuted into rent-charges, 4; the Tithe Commutation Act, the last assertion of State-ownership, 101.

Tithes not voluntary in origin, remarks on the proofs of this, 12, 25, 26, 29, 33, 52–54, 60–64, 78–83.

Vegetables, tithes of, how levied, 44.

Wages, tithes of, 50.
Warburton, Bishop, on Church property, 118.
Waste lands, extent of their enclosure, 56.
Watson, Bishop, on Church property, 118.
Wax, tithes of, how levied, 46.
Western Church the only Church that has resorted to tithes, 9.
William I., law of tithes, 24.
Winchester, parliament of, A.D. 855, 18.
Wood, tithes of, how levied, 41.
Wool, tithes of, how levied, 48.

THE END.

www.ingramcontent.com/pod-product-compliance
Lightning Source LLC
Chambersburg PA
CBHW020249170426
43202CB00008B/293